MEANS AND PROBABILITIES

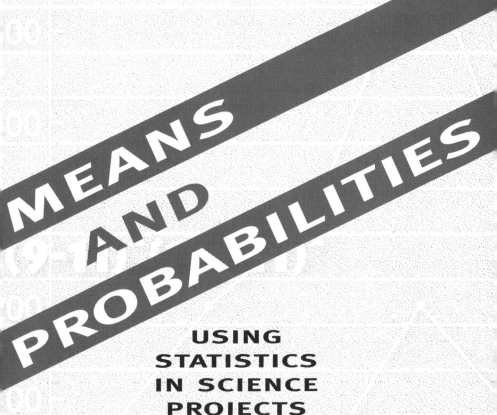

MEANS AND PROBABILITIES

USING STATISTICS IN SCIENCE PROJECTS

BY
MELANIE JACOBS KRIEGER

EXPERIMENTAL SCIENCE

FRANKLIN WATTS
A Division of Grolier Publishing
New York   London   Hong Kong   Sydney
Danbury, Connecticut

*To my husband, Allen,
and my children, Tara and Stevn:
the best statistics in the world!*

Photographs copyright ©: Melanie Jacobs Krieger: pp. 9, 14, 111, 112, 115, 118, 121; Westinghouse Science Talent Search: p. 12; UPI/ Bettmann: p. 18; Unicorn Stock Photos: pp. 21 (Jeff Greenberg/MR), 56 (Ron P. Jaffe), 94 (Eric R. Berndt); Monkmeyer: pp. 28 (Robert Capece), 31, 64, 73 (all Mimi Forsyth), 39 (Grant LeDuc), 49 (Michael Kagan); Transcendental Graphics: pp. 36, 105; Omni-Photo Communications, Inc.: p. 53; Photo Researchers: p. 79 (Sheila Terry/SPL). Electronic pagination: Carole Desnoes

Library of Congress Cataloging-in-Publication Data

Krieger, Melanie Jacobs.
    Means and probabilities : using statistics in science projects by Melanie Jacobs Krieger.
        p. cm. — (Experimental science)
    Includes bibliographical references and index.
    Summary: An introduction to statistics with emphasis on their use in science projects. Explains averages, frequency distribution, range, percentile, probability, standard deviation, and more.
        ISBN 0-531-11225-X
        1. Statistics—Juvenile literature. 2. Science—Experiments—Statistical methods—Juvenile literature. [1. Statistics. 2. Science projects.] I. Title. II. Series: Experimental science series book.
    QA276.13.K75 1996
    001.4'22—dc20   95-49013
                                                                      CIP
                                                                      AC

Copyright © 1996 by Melanie Jacobs Krieger
All rights reserved. Published simultaneously in Canada.
Printed in the United States of America
1 2 3 4 5 6 7 8 9 10 R 05 04 03 02 01 00 99 98 97 96

CONTENTS

INTRODUCTION

People usually think of mathematics as a very exact science. For instance, you can be quite sure that $2 + 2 = 4$. You know that if you had 2 dollars and a friend were to give you another 2 dollars, you would have 4 dollars. The solution to this problem is precise and easily understood. No interpretation is necessary. The basic methods you learn in your math classes enable you to add dollars, inches, miles, and so on to obtain exact values as answers.

However, everything in life is not this simple. Many mathematical problems do not ask you to just add and subtract numbers, but require you to collect, organize, analyze, and interpret numbers. This is when mathematicians turn to statistics for help.

For example, suppose you wanted to know whether the girls in the ninth grade of your school are better spellers than the boys or vice versa. To find out, you would first have to give them all a spelling test.

Table 1. Spelling Scores for Ninth-Graders	
Average Score	
Girls	87
Boys	85

You would then find the average score for each gender. Then you could compare the girls' average score to the boys' average score.

But this is not always so easy. What if your results are as shown in Table 1?

At first glance, you might say that the girls are better spellers than the boys. But if you think about it, you might realize that the scores are really not *that* different. You might begin to wonder whether you could say with certainty that the girls are better spellers than the boys. After all, you could argue that both scores would receive a B$^+$ on a report card. Now you have a dilemma. You have two numbers that are definitely not the same yet are very close in value. Can you say the 2-point difference is meaningful?

This is where statistical methods can help. Statistics can be used to determine whether the difference is meaningful, or significant. Once you learn statistical techniques, you will find that they are easy to use and can help immensely in finding answers to important problems.

Means and Probabilities is a practical, how-to book. It does not derive statistical formulas or explain the mathematics behind the various formulas and methods. It will show you how to use statistics to interpret the data you compile in a science project. You will find that using statistics adds immensely to the conclusions you draw and the impression your project makes on the judges in science competitions.

THE SCIENTIFIC METHOD

Science research experiments can be very exciting projects. Each undertaking is a distinct and unique experience with the possibility of discovering something new and exciting. It may be new not only to you, but also to the science world!

If you have never done a science project, you will find that it is very different from a high school lab project. In the high school lab, the teacher typically assigns a task or a project that lasts about 30 minutes. The correct results of the task are already known by the

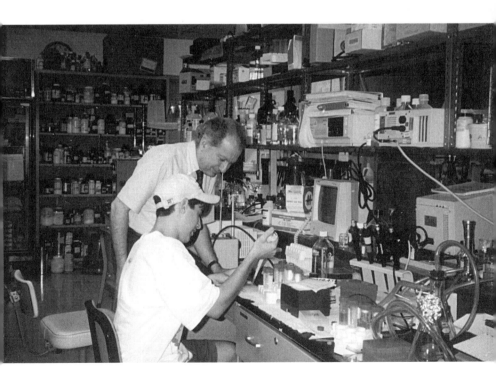

**A student carries out a science project at the
University at Stony Brook in New York.**

teacher, and if your results are different from the expected ones, your experiment is usually considered a failure.

However, real science does not proceed this way. Scientists in the research laboratory do not know what their results will be. They work with hypotheses and unknowns. They seek the unexpected and new. In addition, quite often their experiments meet with failure, rather than success. But this is how science proceeds. Knowing what does not work leads scientists to try new things.

Real scientists do not carry out a series of 30-minute projects. Each project takes as long as necessary—minutes, hours, days, even years. As the experiment progresses, a scientist may revise the hypothesis in response to new information. There is no cookbook recipe as there is in the high school laboratory. A real scientist encounters a great deal of frustration along with success.

A real science project always follows the scientific method. The scientific method is a set of steps all scientists follow when conducting research experiments. If you follow these steps, you can create a science research project that would qualify for any of the prestigious science research competitions, such as the Westinghouse Science Talent Search Competition. It might even be worthy of being published in a scientific journal.

The scientific method involves the following six steps:

1. State a hypothesis.

A hypothesis is a statement asserting the problem you will be investigating in your experiment. As you work on your project, you hope to prove or disprove the statement. For example, a person conducting the spelling investigation discussed earlier might have a hypothesis that girls are better spellers than boys.

Before you come up with a hypothesis, it is a good idea to read all the background information you can about your research topic. Remember to consult current periodicals, journals, and computer databases, as well as books. Try to discover whether or not other people have tried an experiment similar to the one you want to do. If so, look into the results they obtained.

Now you are ready to formulate your own hypothesis. State the problem you will be investigating in your experiment.

2. Design an experiment that will allow you to accept or reject the hypothesis.

Now that you have stated the problem, decide on the type of data you will need to collect and how you will go about gathering it.

Start by writing an outline of the procedures you plan to use. Write up a tentative schedule; then think about the equipment and lab setup you will need. Determine whether you must buy or borrow special apparatus and whether you will have to construct a special lab setup. If you will be working with live specimens, such as plants, determine where you will store them and how you will care for them.

If your research involves vertebrate animals, human subjects, recombinant DNA, or animal tissue, learn the rules and fill out the appropriate forms for conducting research in these areas. Discover the safety measures that you must take with your experiment. For projects involving human subjects, find out if you will need consent forms.

For projects in the social sciences, develop your

Development of a Novel Choline Oxidase-Chemiluminescent Detection System and Its Potential Use in Phospholipase D- and Immunodetection Assays

DATA & RESULTS

MATERIALS & METHODS

questionnaire and define the subject pool you wish to test.

Remember to design your experiment so that only one variable at a time is being changed or tested. In this way, you can be certain that any change in outcome is caused by the variable and nothing else. If too many things are changing at the same time, you will never be able to understand how the variable you tested affects the end result.

3. Assemble the experimental setup.

Assemble the equipment for your experiment. First, hook up and test your newly purchased equipment and other hardware to make sure you can conduct your experiment without frequent breakdowns.

If you are doing a project in the social sciences, create a survey form that you can use to question participants.

4. Conduct your experiment and collect the data.

The *data* are the numbers you collect during your project. For instance, it may be the number of french fries in a fast-food serving or the number of inches of rainfall per day. If your project involves a questionnaire, this is the time to give out the questionnaire and collect the responses. The responses will be your data.

In carrying out your experiment, carefully follow the procedures you have planned. Do not be alarmed if you run into a number of problems with the equip-

Deborah Yeh of Plano, Texas, won fifth place in the 1995 Westinghouse Talent Search.

**Science projects involving plants may
require special setup and care.**

ment or lab setup. When that happens, simply make
modifications to your original plan. Your persever-
ance and ingenuity in solving these problems will
demonstrate your talent as a scientist.

5. Analyze the data, using statistical methods.

Analyze and interpret the data you have collected from your experiment. First, organize your data,
using tables, charts, and graphs. Then, using the sta-

tistical methods explained in this book, interpret the data. Your analysis will enable you to make a scientific judgment as to whether you have proved or disproved your original hypothesis.

You can carry out your statistical analysis with a calculator or one of the commercial statistical computer packages.

6. Write and publish the paper.

Your work is not complete until you write up your results and share them with other scientists and researchers.

The advantage of the scientific method is that it allows you to develop a hypothesis and then prove it or disprove it in a logical and straightforward manner. Statistics is an essential part of this process. It allows you to analyze and interpret the data you collect during the course of your experiment.

UNDERSTANDING STATISTICS

This book will start by showing you how to arrange data in graphs and charts. You will then learn to calculate averages and other *descriptive statistics.* Descriptive statistics are values that describe some aspect of the data. Later, you will learn about statistics that help interpret data. They are called *inferential statistics* because they allow you to make inferences, or conclusions, about a large group of objects or people from your investigation of only a small sample of the group.

In most cases, it is impossible to study the entire group, or *population*, in an experiment. If you were studying a particular plant or animal, for example, you would not be able to study every one that exists in the world. If you attend a very large school, it might be difficult to test the spelling ability of all the ninth-graders in your school. But you could choose a *sample* of students that you believe represents the entire population of ninth-graders. For example, you would want to include students from both the honors and nonhonors classes to ensure that all levels of ability are included in your sample.

If the sample is to accurately represent the entire population, it is very important that the items or individuals in the sample be chosen randomly. The easiest way to do this for the spelling investigation would be to assign a number to every ninth grader. Then you would put all the numbers in a container, shake it up, and pull out numbers at random. A computer can also help you select random numbers.

The best way to learn statistical methods is to actually apply them to different problems. For that reason, there are many examples throughout the book. As you go through the examples, think about how the same techniques might be applied to your own projects.

ORGANIZING DATA

Collecting data is an important aspect of every science project. It may sound like a simple thing to do, but if it is not done in a neat and organized manner, you may find it frustrating, if not impossible, to analyze and interpret your data. The best way to organize your data is to put it into a table.

Suppose you are measuring the acidity of the rainfall in your town from day to day. Your data table might look like Table 2.

A properly constructed table clearly summarizes

Table 2. Data for Rainfall Experiment

	Rainfall, inches	Ph
Day 1	0.11	5.5
Day 2	0.34	4.5

**Which is the tallest mountain: Mount Everest (left),
Mount Lhotse (center), or Mount Nuptse (right)?**

a set of data. It presents information far more effectively than a sentence full of numbers.

For instance, what if you wanted to list the five tallest mountains, with their locations and heights? If you wrote all this information in a sentence, you might have something like this:

The five tallest mountains in the world are: Mount Everest at 29,108 feet in the Himalayan Mountain Range in Nepal and Tibet; Mount Godwin Austin at 29,064 feet in the Karakoram Mountain Range in Kashmir; Mount Kanchenjunga at 28,208 feet in the Himalayan Mountain Range in Nepal and Sikkim; Mount Lhotse at 27,890 feet in the Himalayan Mountain Range in Nepal and Tibet; and Mount Makalu at 27,790 feet in the Himalayan Mountain Range in Nepal and Tibet.

This sentence contains a lot of information about the five tallest mountains in the world, but the information is difficult to grasp quickly. You cannot easily see the relationship among the pieces of information. For instance, the following is not immediately obvious:

- The name of the tallest mountain in the world
- The location of the second tallest mountain
- The name of the mountain(s) found in Sikkim

Table 3 organizes all the information found in the sentence. The table was easier to create than the long clumsy sentence, and it is much easier to understand. You can immediately see that:

- The tallest mountain is Mount Everest, with an elevation of 29,108 feet.

Table 3. The Five Tallest Mountains in the World

Mountain	Elevation (in feet)	Location
Mount Everest	29,108	Himalayas in Nepal and Tibet
Mount Godwin Austin	29,064	Karakoram Mountains in Kashmir
Mount Kanchenjunga	28,208	Himalayas in Nepal and Sikkim
Mount Lhotse	27,890	Himalayas in Nepal and Tibet
Mount Makalu	27,790	Himalayas in Nepal and Tibet

- The second tallest mountain, Mount Godwin Austin is found in the Karakoram Mountains in Kashmir.
- Mount Kanchenjunga is the mountain found in Sikkim.

You can also quickly see that four of the tallest mountains in the world are in the Himalayas. And with a quick calculation you can determine that the difference between the world's tallest mountain and the fifth tallest mountain is only 1,318 feet.

By the time you finish your science project, you will have collected a large amount of data. At first glance, your data values may appear random and spread out. Most likely, you will not have an instant picture of your experimental results. But if you arrange these numbers into a table or chart, you will have a format that is simple and easy to read.

A table will summarize the data and show you its *distribution,* or how your data is spread out over a range of values. Thus, you will be able to see clusterings and trends in the data. At a glance, you will be able to see the scores at the extremes and in the center of your distribution.

A table should be a self-contained body of information. All the columns must be clearly labeled and the title should be self-explanatory. This makes it possible to understand the results of the experiment just by reading the title and then studying the table.

Each table you create is different depending on the type and the amount of data you have collected. Suppose you had surveyed 15 customers chosen ran-

How many CDs do most customers buy?

Table 4. The Number of CDs Bought by Customers

Number of CDs per customer	1	2	3	4	5
Number of customers	5	4	3	2	1

domly at Dave's Music Discs to find out how many compact discs they were buying. You might end up with the following 15 pieces of data:

1, 4, 5, 3, 2, 1, 4, 3, 2, 2, 1, 1, 2, 1, 3

This string of numbers is rather meaningless until you organize it in a table. Table 4 summarizes the data. If you examine the table briefly, it is fairly obvious that most customers bought 1 or 2 CDs.

GROUPING DATA

In many experiments, you may collect hundreds of pieces of data. A large number of values widely spread out can be unwieldy to work with. In such situations, it is often helpful to arrange the data in groups.

To demonstrate the advantage of this approach, let's take an example with 40 pieces of data. Suppose you wish to assess the mathematics abilities of the students in your high school by using scores on the math portion of the Scholastic Aptitude Test (SAT I).

You might go to the high school guidance office and randomly select 40 student files. The high school should withhold the identities of the students. It is best not to have this information so that you can remain objective. Simply record the 40 math SAT I scores as shown in Table 5.

As you look at these numbers, you will likely find that you are unable to determine anything about the

Table 5. Math SAT I Scores of 40 High School Students

770	670	580	720	680	500	520	610	500	490
600	560	600	570	610	630	700	500	540	640
560	550	650	670	640	530	520	580	610	600
470	650	570	600	550	660	640	510	520	500

Note: The lowest possible Math SAT I score is 200 and the highest possible score is 800.

math abilities of the students in your high school. Table 5 gives no indication of the average score. But if you organize the scores in some logical way, they will have more meaning.

One approach is to list all possible scores beginning with the highest and ending with the lowest of the 40 scores. Since SAT I scores are always multiples of 10, the list will include all multiples of 10 from 470 to 770. If you place a slash mark next to each score every time it appears in Table 5, you will be able to see the distribution of scores. The number of slash marks represents the frequency of each score. See Table 6.

Table 6 is called an ungrouped *frequency distribution* of scores. Although you can now see that the data is spread widely among the scores in the table, the table still does not indicate in any way the average score. Grouping the scores into categories, known as *class intervals*, will give you a better idea of where the average is and how the scores are distributed.

For this example, a good choice for the number of groups is 10. First, find the highest score in the list—770—and the lowest score in the list—470—and subtract the two:

$$770 - 470 = 300$$

Table 6. Frequency Distribution of Math SAT I scores of 40 High School Students

Scores

770	/	660	/	550	/ /
760		650	/ /	540	/
750		640	/ / /	530	/
740		630	/	520	/ / /
730		620		510	/
720	/	610	/ / /	500	/ / / /
710		600	/ / / /	490	/
700	/	590		480	
690		580	/ /	470	/
680	/	570	/ /		
670	/ /	560	/ /		

There is a 300-point spread between the lowest and highest scores in this distribution. This spread is called the *range*.

Divide the range by 10, the number of categories, to find how many SAT I points each group will cover.

$$300/10 = 30$$

Each class interval will cover 30 points. The first interval will range from a lower limit of 470 to an upper limit of 499. Notice that the difference between the upper and lower limit is only 29, but the number of points in the range is 30. If you have any doubt about this, count the points yourself. The next interval starts at 500 and ends at 529.

Find the remaining intervals by continuing this procedure of incrementing 1 for the lower limit and then adding 29 to the lower limit to get the upper limit.

[24]

Table 7. Class Intervals for Math SAT I Scores

Row Value	Lower Limit	Upper Limit
10	740 − 770
9	710 − 739
8	680 − 709
7	650 − 679
6	620 − 649
5	590 − 619
4	560 − 589
3	530 − 559
2	500 − 529
1	470 − 499

Now list the ten groups vertically in decreasing order as shown in Table 7. Notice that the last interval will have to contain 31 points to include 770.

Follow this general procedure whenever you are creating class intervals. It is always easier to start with the bottom interval and go up. Adding to a lower limit rather than subtracting from an upper limit will help you avoid careless mathematical errors.

To complete the grouped frequency distribution, mark the number of scores in each interval with slashes as in Table 6. Write the total number of slashes in a new column as shown in Table 8. This number is the frequency count in each interval. It is a good idea to check your work by adding up the frequency counts to make sure you have included all 40 data points.

The spread of the scores becomes much more obvious with this grouped frequency distribution. You can see that most of the scores are clustered in the first seven rows—the middle and lower end of the score

Table 8. Grouped Frequency Distribution for Math SAT I Scores

Row Value	Lower Limit	Upper Limit	Tally	Frequency, f
10	740	770	/	1
9	710	739	/	1
8	680	709	/ /	2
7	650	679	/ / / / /	5
6	620	649	/ / / /	4
5	590	619	/ / / / / / /	7
4	560	589	/ / / / / /	6
3	530	559	/ / / /	4
2	500	529	/ / / / / / / /	8
1	470	499	/ /	2
			Total	40

range. But the last three rows, representing the highest scores, have only one or two scores apiece.

Thus, the table displays the basic characteristics and trends of the SAT I score distribution while also summarizing the data.

For any given situation, you must choose the number of classes based mainly on the amount of raw data you have. In most cases, it is best to put your data in anywhere from 10 to 20 groups. You want enough classes to show the spread of your data; if the intervals are too large, you risk losing too much information. Differences in the values of the original data are lost when the numbers are lumped together.

But if there are too many groups, the amount of information can be overwhelming. Too many groups defeats the purpose of grouping the data—to easily read, understand, and interpret your data.

A MORE PRECISE FREQUENCY TABLE

There are several other statistical values that can help you define and interpret a frequency distribution. You can add this information to your frequency table by including several extra columns. The values in the columns will allow you to interpret your data in a more precise way, as well as to make accurate graphs of your data.

One helpful piece of information is called *true limits*. The true limits of a measured value are the lower and upper bounds of the measurement. If you weigh yourself on a scale, for instance, it may read 100 pounds, but do you really weigh exactly 100 pounds? Because of imperfections in the construction of the scale, you may weigh a bit more or a bit less than 100 pounds.

How much more or less? If the scale display has increments of one pound, then you could weigh anywhere from 99.5 to 100.5 pounds and still get a reading of 100 pounds. These are the true limits of your weight measurements. Thus the true limits of a measurement can be obtained by taking half of the smallest increment on the scale display, and then both subtracting and adding that value to the measurement value.

True limits are usually listed with class intervals as shown in Table 9.

Another valuable statistic is the *midpoint* of the

Table 9. Examples of True Limits for Class Intervals

Class Intervals	True Limits
38 − 53	37.5 − 53.5
22.3 − 26.3	22.25 − 26.35

Table 10. The Midpoints of Some Class Intervals

Interval	Midpoint
4 − 6	5
85 − 91	88
123 − 130	126.5

class. It is simply the center of the class interval, and can be calculated by adding the lower and upper class limits and dividing by 2. Because the midpoint is often used to represent the entire class, it is sometimes called the *class mark*. The midpoints of some class intervals are given in Table 10.

In the example with the SAT I test scores, you figured the frequency of data values in each isolated class interval. Sometimes it is helpful to know how these frequencies accumulate as you progress from the lowest class to the highest. The statistic known as the *cumulative frequency*, or *cum f*, supplies this information. It is the sum of all the frequencies from the lowest class up to and including a given class. Table 11 shows the cumulative frequencies for a series of class intervals.

For the first class at the bottom of the table, the cumulative frequency is equal to the frequency, 8, because there are no lower classes. The cumulative frequency of the second class is $8 + 10 = 18$. For the third class, *cum f* $= 18 + 5 = 23$, and so on. You will dis-

The reading you get on a weight scale may differ slightly from your actual weight depending on the true limits of the measurement.

Table 11. The Cumulative Frequencies of a Series of Classes

Class Interval	Midpoint	f	cum f
17 − 20	18.5	10	40
13 − 16	14.5	7	30
9 − 12	10.5	5	23
5 − 8	6.5	10	18
1 − 4	2.5	8	8

cover how useful the cumulative frequency can be in the section on percentiles beginning on p. 48.

The general procedure for organizing any set of data into a frequency distribution table with the columns of Table 11 is as follows:

1. Choose the number of categories, classes, or intervals.
2. Find a convenient class or interval width.
3. Determine the lower and upper interval limits.
4. Determine the true limits for each interval.
5. Determine the midpoint of each interval.
6. Tally the data in the intervals.
7. Determine the frequency for each class.
8. Put the data in a table and add a cumulative frequency column.

Now let's apply this procedure to a large set of data. Suppose you were interested in discovering how 100 randomly selected students performed on the last science test. The grades are shown in Table 12.

The first step is to divide the scores into 10 class intervals. Since the largest score is 99 and the smallest value is 0, the spread of data is 99. If you divide 99

How did 100 students do on the last science test?

Table 12. Science Scores for 100 Students

12	34	56	78	90	11	0	65	75	87
98	21	53	73	82	43	91	95	63	99
54	58	97	32	47	21	38	12	97	32
76	78	98	87	84	83	48	79	94	84
94	93	99	56	86	82	82	91	73	59
33	56	78	93	84	87	85	82	98	54
76	93	98	83	89	82	72	28	59	27
56	78	93	93	97	89	88	77	70	68
76	87	82	81	99	95	96	68	39	60
87	50	39	93	84	78	40	73	79	94

by 10 and round to the nearest whole number, you get a class width of 10.

Thus, the lower class limits will be: 0, 10, 20, . . . 90. And the upper class limits will be: 9, 19, 29, . . . 99.

To determine the true limits for these classes, you must know how the science teacher scored the tests. Let's assume that the teacher gave full-point credits for individual questions. The true limits would then be -0.5 − 9.5, 9.5 − 19.5, 19.5 − 29.5, and so on. Note that the upper class limit of the lowest class is equal to the lower class limit of the next class. This will become very important in Chapter 2 when you graph your data.

To determine the midpoint of each class, subtract the lower class limit from the upper class limit and divide by 2: $(9 − 0)/2 = 4.5$. Therefore, 4.5 is the class mark, or midpoint, of the first interval. Note that even though 4.5 is the representative score for this interval, a score of 4.5 is not possible. Continue in the same way to find the midpoint of the other classes.

Tally the number of scores in each class and total them to obtain a frequency for each class interval. Then calculate the cumulative frequency for each class. You should now be able to organize your data into a table as shown in Table 13.

If you study Table 13, you can see the entire distribution of scores. At a glance, you can tell the location of the extreme and central scores of your distribution. You can see that there are very few scores between 0 and 29 and many scores between 70 and 99. In fact, this distribution of scores is very lopsided. Most of the scores are clustered above 70 instead of in the middle of the distribution around the score of 50.

Thus, the frequency distribution table summarized the experimental results and displayed the basic characteristics and trends of the data. A teacher would

Table 13. Frequency Distribution of 100 Students on a Science Test

Class	Class Limits	True Limits	Midpoint	f	Cum f
10	90 – 99	89.5 – 99.5	94.5	25	100
9	80 – 89	79.5 – 89.5	84.5	23	75
8	70 – 79	69.5 – 79.5	74.5	17	52
7	60 – 69	59.5 – 69.5	64.5	5	35
6	50 – 59	49.5 – 59.5	54.5	11	30
5	40 – 49	39.5 – 49.5	44.5	4	19
4	30 – 39	29.5 – 39.5	34.5	7	15
3	20 – 29	19.5 – 29.5	24.5	4	8
2	10 – 19	9.5 – 19.5	14.5	3	4
1	0 – 9	-0.5 – 9.5	4.5	1	1

find this information valuable because it could help pinpoint the best score to choose as the passing grade. For instance, if 60 were the passing grade, 70 of the 100 students would pass the test. This can be determined by summing all the frequencies from class 7 and higher, since 60 is the lower limit of class 7. Adding all the frequencies in class 7 and up would give you: 5 + 17 + 23 + 25 = 70. Or you could simply subtract the cumulative frequency for class 6 from 100. Can you see why this works?

Next, the frequency distribution will be used as the basis for constructing several types of graphs that will help you visually interpret your data.

GRAPHING DATA

In contrast to a table, a graph summarizes data from an experiment in a pictorial way. A pictorial presentation of data often exposes certain features that are not apparent in a frequency table. There are many types of graphs. Stem-and-leaf diagrams, pie charts, bar graphs, histograms, and frequency polygons are some of the more common. You must decide which one is best suited for your application.

As with tables, every graph needs a self-explanatory title, and the data must be clearly labeled.

STEM-AND-LEAF DIAGRAMS

Stem-and-leaf diagrams let you quickly see the shape or the spread of your data. Compared with other types of graphs, a unique feature of stem-and-leaf diagrams is that they include the actual numerical values of the collected data.

As an example, let's construct a stem-and-leaf diagram of the number of home runs Babe Ruth hit in each of his 15 years with the New York Yankees. Beginning with the year 1920 and ending with 1934, those values are:

54 59 35 41 46 25 47 60 54 46 49 46 41 34 22

To make a stem-and-leaf diagram, first arrange the numbers in increasing order. Then separate each piece of data into the 10's digit and the 1's digit. The 10's digits will form the stems of the diagram and the 1's digits will form the leaves.

List each stem value on one line with the leaves to the right. For instance, a stem value of 2 would have two leaves to the right because there are two data values in the 20s: 22 and 25. So the leaves would be 2 and 5. It is best to arrange the leaves in increasing order, as shown in Figure 1. Also, separate the stems and leaves with a vertical line.

10's digits	1's digits
2	2 5
3	4 5
4	1 1 6 6 6 7 9
5	4 4 9
6	0

Figure 1. A stem-and-leaf diagram arranges the yearly number of home runs Babe Ruth hit from 1920 to 1934 according to 10's digits.

Babe Ruth hits one of 60 home runs in 1927.

From the stem-and-leaf diagram, you can immediately see that the range of home runs is from 22 to 60. The smallest number of runs is 22, and the largest number is 60. You can also see that stem 6 contains the fewest number of leaves. It has just one leaf. That tells you that Babe Ruth had only one season in which he hit 60 or more home runs.

Stem 4, with 7 leaves, contains the most leaves. This means that most of the data is concentrated in the 40s. Babe Ruth hit between 40 and 50 home runs during seven seasons of play. The center of the distribution, 46, is located on stem 4. It is the point at which there are an equal number of data points above and below it. Babe Ruth hit less than 46 home runs six of the years, more than 46 six of the years, and exactly 46 three of the years. So it is readily apparent that this group of data is centered at 46.

You can easily see the overall shape of the distribution, which is determined by how far the leaves extend to the right. The shape for this set of data is relatively *symmetric*. A distribution is symmetric if the portions above and below its center are mirror images of each other. In this case, the distribution is not quite symmetric because the two upper stems have 2 leaves apiece, whereas the two lower stems have 3 and 1. If a distribution is far from being symmetric, it is *skewed*.

The diagram also shows that there are no gaps in the distribution, nor are there any *outliers*. An outlier is an extreme score that falls far outside the overall pattern of the data. An outlier could indicate an error—in recording the data, for instance—or it may simply represent a very unusual occurrence.

A stem-and-leaf diagram with an outlier is shown in Figure 2. It displays the number of home runs Roger Maris hit during his 10 years in the American League. The outlier is the 61 home runs he hit in 1961. This

```
0 | 8
1 | 3  4  6
2 | 3  6  8
3 | 3  9
4 |
5 |
6 | 1
```

Figure 2. A stem-and-leaf diagram shows Roger Maris's yearly home runs during 10 years in the American League.

was an extraordinary year for him, since in most years he hit less than half that many. So Maris's record year is an outlier, an individual value that stands apart from his usual pattern.

BAR GRAPHS

Bar graphs consist of either vertical or horizontal bars. The length of each bar represents the number of items in a category. Thus, the graph allows you to visually compare quantities. Suppose you want to display the voting pattern of a random sample of 100 voters taken during the election for mayor of Florida City. The results of the sample are shown in Table 14.

Table 14. Votes of 100 Randomly Chosen Voters in Florida City Mayoral Election

Candidates	Votes
Brown	25
Cho	41
Rivera	34

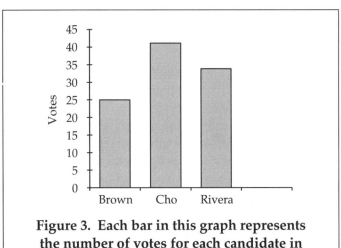

Figure 3. Each bar in this graph represents the number of votes for each candidate in a Florida City mayoral election.

The choices voters make during an election can be presented visually in a bar graph.

A bar graph of these results would look like Figure 3. This presentation allows you to see clearly and immediately the differences in the number of votes for each candidate. Note that the length of the bar represents the quantity you wish to compare. The bars must be of uniform width and equally spaced. Note also that the bars are separated rather than touching. Bar graphs are suitable for situations in which the data "values" are not of a continuous numerical nature, but are completely separate items, such as the names of candidates in an election.

HISTOGRAMS

A histogram is similar to a bar graph, but it is designed for data that covers a continuous range of numerical values. As a result, a histogram differs from a bar graph in two important ways. In a histogram the bars always touch, whereas in a bar graph, they are separated. Secondly, you can make the bars in a bar graph as wide as you wish to make the visual impression you want to convey. But in a histogram, the width of a bar represents a numerical value.

A histogram of the number of home runs that Babe Ruth hit in each of his 15 years with the New York Yankees is shown in Figure 4.

Notice that the histogram shows the shape of the distribution in the same way the stem-and-leaf diagram did. The stem-and-leaf diagram is somewhat like a histogram turned on its side.

To create a histogram:

1. Divide the range of data into classes of equal width.
2. Count the number of observations in each class.
3. Draw the histogram.

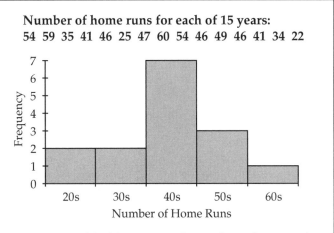

Number of home runs for each of 15 years:
54 59 35 41 46 25 47 60 54 46 49 46 41 34 22

Figure 4. This histogram shows how frequently Babe Ruth's yearly number of home runs fell into each class interval.

The histogram gives the impression that frequencies jump suddenly from one class to the next. If you want to emphasize the continuous rise or fall of the frequencies, you can easily convert the histogram into a frequency polygon or line graph.

FREQUENCY POLYGONS

A frequency polygon might be thought of as a histogram that has been turned into a line graph. It is made by connecting the midpoints of the tops of the bars of the histogram. But a frequency polygon can be constructed without first drawing a histogram. Just plot the frequency of each class at the midpoint of the interval and connect the points.

A frequency polygon of Babe Ruth's home runs is plotted in Figure 5.

Frequency polygons are especially useful for comparing two different distributions. The frequency poly-

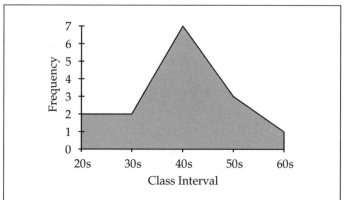

Figure 5. This frequency polygon shows the shape of the distribution of Babe Ruth's yearly home runs from 1920 to 1934.

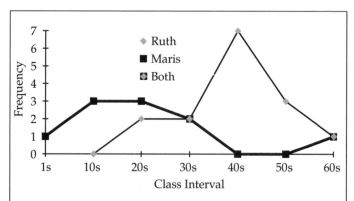

Figure 6. The frequency polygon for Babe Ruth's home run record from 1920 to 1934 (diamonds) is compared with the frequency polygon for Roger Maris's home run record during his 10 years in the American League (squares).

gon in Figure 6, for example, compares the number of home runs hit by Babe Ruth and Roger Maris.

PIE CHART

A graph drawn in the shape of a circle is known as a pie chart. Pie charts can be grasped quickly, and they can give a good overview of your collected data. They are especially useful for showing the component parts of a quantity.

The total quantity—100%—is represented by the entire circle. Each wedge or pie slice of the circle represents some percentage of the total. A pie chart of Babe Ruth's home run record is shown in Figure 7. It was created by first converting the frequency counts to percentages of the total number of years, as shown

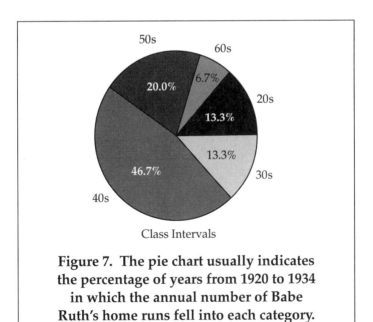

Class Intervals

Figure 7. The pie chart usually indicates the percentage of years from 1920 to 1934 in which the annual number of Babe Ruth's home runs fell into each category.

Table 15. Figuring the Pie Slices

Raw Scores	Percentages	Degrees
20's: 2	2/15 = 13.3%	.133 × 360 = 47.88°
30's: 2	2/15 = 13.3%	.133 × 360 = 47.88°
40's: 7	7/15 = 46.7%	.467 × 360 = 168.12°
50's: 3	3/15 = 20.0%	.200 × 360 = 72.00°
60's: 1	1/15 = 6.7%	.067 × 360 = 24.12°
$n = 15$	Total: 100%	Total: 360°

in Table 15. Multiplying these percentages by 360° then gives the size of the pie slice in degrees.

To construct a pie chart:

1. Change each score to a percentage.
2. Multiply each percentage by 360 (the number of degrees in a circle) to obtain the number of degrees to assign to each component.
3. Use a protractor to mark off each component on the pie chart.
4. Label each segment with the corresponding percentage of the total.

DESCRIPTIVE STATISTICS

An average is a way of representing a set of data by a single descriptive number. It is one of many descriptive statistics. But the term *average* can be deceptive. For instance, what is the average of the following five science test scores?

$$100, \ 100, \ 80, \ 40, \ 30$$

You might be inclined to say the average is 70. However, another person could look at the same set of data and say the average score is 80. And yet a third could say it is 100! And all three would be right! How can that be? The word *average* really has three different definitions, all having to do with measures of central tendency. They are called the *mean*, the *median*, and the *mode*.

When most people say "average," they are referring to the mean. The mean is the total sum of the numbers divided by the quantity of numbers. For the science test scores, you would have:

$$\frac{100 + 100 + 80 + 40 + 30}{5} = \frac{350}{5} = 70$$

The formula for the mean is

$$\bar{x} = \frac{\Sigma x}{n},$$

where Σ is a mathematical symbol meaning "sum," x represents the data, and n is the number of data values. The symbol for the mean, $\bar{x}$, is pronounced "x bar."

The mean is very sensitive to a single extreme score. If the lowest science test score of 30 were replaced with a score of 0, then you would have the following:

100, 100, 80, 40, 0

The mean would become 64, a drop of 6 points! The mean is similarly affected by a single very high score.

The median is the number found in the middle position in your list of values. For the science test scores, the median is 80 because it is the score in the middle of the list. When you have many pieces of data, it is best to arrange them in order and to assign each one a position, as follows:

Positions: (1) (2) (3) (4) (5)
Scores: 100 100 80 40 30

The position numbers help you find the middle score. When there are an odd number of scores, the middle-position number is always half of the number following the highest-position number. So in this list, 3 is the middle-position number.

Finding the median for an even number of scores is not so straightforward. You must calculate the arithmetic mean of the two middle scores. Suppose you have the following six scores:

Positions:	(1)	(2)	(3)	(4)	(5)	(6)
Scores:	100	100	80	70	40	30

The median is the mean of the two middle scores, which are in positions 3 and 4. Therefore the median would be 75.

The median is a good average to use when there is a single extreme or indeterminate score. For instance, suppose your experiment involves timing mice as they run through a maze. After you have timed five mice, the sixth mouse refuses to run the maze. To find the average running time, you should include all the scores. But if you include the sixth mouse's time as 0, it will throw your average running time off. The median will give you a pretty accurate average running time, even with the aberrant piece of data.

The mode is the value or score that appears the most often in your list of data. The value 100 appears twice in the list of science scores, and the values 80, 40, and 30 appear only once. The number 100 is the mode of the five test scores because it appears most often. The mode is appropriate for projects in which it is important to find the most common value in the distribution. Although it is not true for this example, the mode can also give a quick, rough estimate of central tendency.

Sometimes two values appear in a list of scores the exact same number of times. If each occurs more often than any other value, then you have what is called a *bimodal* distribution. And if more than two values appear in your list the most number of times, you have a *multimodal* distribution.

The mode is easy to compute, but as you have seen it can be very far from what most people consider average.

PERCENTILES

A data value by itself is meaningless. It takes on meaning only when it is compared with the rest of the values in the data set.

Suppose your sister announced, "I received a score of 156 on my chemistry aptitude test." What would your reaction be? Would you commend her for a fine score or would you criticize her for not getting a higher score? Or would you reserve judgment until you learned more about the scores of the other students in your sister's class? Of course, that would be the wisest course.

If your sister told you, "Eighty-seven percentage of the students scored the same or lower than I did," she would be providing some frame of reference for interpreting the score. Indeed, she would have been telling you the *percentile rank* of her score.

The percentile rank of a score is the percentage of scores in a tested population, or group, that are equal to or lower than the score. So if your sister said her score of 156 had a percentile rank of 87, she would be saying that 87 percent of her classmates scored 156 or lower on the chemistry aptitude test. With this information, you would know that she did very well.

The most obvious way to calculate percentile rankings is to rank the scores in increasing order, and then calculate the percentage of scores at or below a given score.

If your sister said she scored in the 87th percentile on a chemistry test, how well did she do?

Examine, for instance, the following list of ten chemistry grades ranked in increasing order:

Rank: (1) (2) (3) (4) (5) (6) (7) (8) (9) (10)
Score: 68   76   77   80   80   80   85   88   90   94

If you wanted to calculate the percentile rank of the score 77, you would note that there are 3 scores less than or equal to 77. Three scores out of ten scores translates to a percentage of 30. The percentile rank of the score 77 is 30 percent; in other words, 30 percent of the grades are at or below 77.

Table 16. Cumulative Frequency Distribution

Score	f	cum (f)
94	1	10
90	1	9
88	1	8
85	1	7
80	3	6
77	1	3
76	1	2
68	1	1

The percentile rank can also be determined directly from a cumulative frequency table. Table 16 displays the cumulative frequency distribution of the ten chemistry grades.

If you wanted to know the percentile rank of the score 80, you could simply look up its cumulative frequency in the table. A cumulative frequency of 6 means that 6 out of 10, or 60 percent, of the grades are at or below 80. You can use the following equation to calculate percentile rank if you know the cumulative frequency:

$$\text{Percentile Rank} = \frac{cum\,f}{n} \times 100$$

where n is the total number of scores or data values.

The calculation of percentile rank for the score of 90 is as follows:

$$\text{Percentile Rank} = \frac{cum\,f}{n} \times 100$$

$$\text{P. R.} = \frac{9}{10} \times 100$$

$$= 90\%$$

SPECIAL PERCENTILES

For convenience, percentiles are sometimes divided into subsets. *Deciles*, for example, break percentiles into 10 groups of 10 percentage points each. The first decile is equivalent to the 10th percentile, and the ninth decile is equal to the 90th percentile. Schools often give the scores for standardized tests of mathematics and reading in the form of deciles. SAT I test scores also include deciles.

Quartiles break up the range of percentiles into fourths. The first quartile, Q_1, is the 25th percentile; the second quartile, Q_2, is the 50th percentile; and the third quartile, Q_3, is the 75th percentile. Note that the second quartile, Q_2, is the median of the data.

Suppose you wanted to find the quartiles for the following set of golf scores from 11 members of a high school golf team participating in match play:

89 90 87 95 86 81 102 105 83 88 91

First, rank the data from smallest to largest:

(1)	(2)	(3)	(4)	(5)	(6)	(7)	(8)	(9)	(10)	(11)
81	83	86	87	88	89	90	91	95	102	105

Then find the median by choosing the middle position—in this case (6). This defines the second quartile; Q_2 is 89. To find the first quartile, find the median of the lower half of the data. This includes only the data that is less than the median, as follows:

(1)	(2)	(3)	(4)	(5)
81	83	86	8	88

The median for these scores is position (3). Thus, the first quartile score is 86.

Now find the median of the upper half of the data to get the third quartile. The upper half of the data is:

(7) (8) (9) (10) (11)
90 91 95 102 105

The median for these scores is position (9). Thus, the third quartile score is 95.

To summarize, the quartile values for the golf team members are:

$$Q_1: 86 \quad Q_2: 89 \quad Q_3: 95$$

There are many ways to calculate quartiles, but most people use the following general method:

1. Rank the data from smallest to largest.
2. Find the median. This is the second quartile, Q_2.
3. Find the median of the lower half of the data. This will be the first quartile, Q_1.
4. Find the median of the upper half of the data. This will be the third quartile, Q_3.

FIVE-NUMBER SUMMARIES AND BOXPLOTS

It is often convenient to include the minimum and maximum values with the quartiles to quickly summarize a distribution. This is called a *five-number summary*. Thus, the five-number summary of the golf scores is:

81, 86, 89, 95, 105

Note that the numbers are given in increasing order, so that you can see at a glance the spread and shape of the data. You can tell that most of the scores are concentrated in the 80s, with the best score at 81 and the worst score at 105. Remember that in golf, the goal is to score low.

Let's find the five-number summary of another set of data. Suppose a marketing consultant wanted to get an idea of how much money shoppers spent at a grocery store. She observes 11 shoppers at the store's

A survey of a random sample of grocery shoppers can indicate their spending patterns.

checkout lanes and records their expenditures, rounded to the nearest dollar, in increasing order as follows:

(1)	(2)	(3)	(4)	(5)	(6)	(7)	(8)	(9)	(10)	(11)
2	10	11	12	15	18	20	24	27	43	64

Minimum spent: 2
First quartile, Q_1:   11
Second quartile, Q_2:   18
Third quartile, Q_3:   27
Maximum spent: 64

Thus, the five-number summary is: 2, 11, 18, 27, 64. It gives a quick overview of the grocery spending patterns of the random sample of customers.

You can absorb the information of the five-number summary more easily if you put it in a *boxplot,* which is essentially a visual representation of the summary. The boxplot for the grocery expenditures is drawn in Figure 8. The five scores are plotted on a vertical scale, and a box is drawn from Q_1 to Q_3 to emphasize where most of the data is found.

Notice that a horizontal line is drawn through the box at Q_2 and that vertical lines extend from the box to the minimum and maximum. These vertical lines are known as *whiskers.* The box shows you where most of the scores are concentrated, and the whiskers show the extremes of the data. This gives you an idea of the shape of the distribution in much the same way a stem-and-leaf diagram does. But in contrast to a stem-and-leaf diagram, a boxplot can display very large sets of data.

To make a boxplot summary:

1. Draw a vertical scale that includes your range of data.

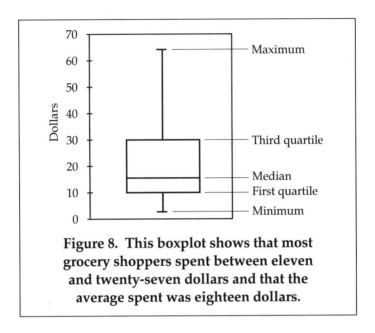

Figure 8. This boxplot shows that most grocery shoppers spent between eleven and twenty-seven dollars and that the average spent was eighteen dollars.

2. To the right of the scale, draw a box of any width from Q_1 to Q_3.
3. Draw a horizontal line through the box at Q_2.
4. Draw lines, or whiskers, from Q_1 to the lowest value and from Q_3 to the highest value.

DISPERSION: THE SPREAD OF THE SCORES

An average is a very important statistic, one that scientists invariably rely on in analyzing data. It is very powerful because it can summarize a set of data with just one number. But without other statistics, an average can sometimes be misleading.

To see this for yourself, imagine that you have a friend, Ellen, who has a craving for chocolate candy bars with nuts. You want to surprise her for her birth-

How many nuts are in each candy bar?

day with a whole case of candy bars. But Ellen is very particular; she likes exactly 40 nuts in each bar.

Which brand should you buy to guarantee that she will be satisfied? You have three brands to choose from: X, Y, and Z. You decide to write to the companies and question them about the average number of nuts in each bar.

Each company writes back with the requested information, along with a complimentary random sample of several of its candy bars. The information

Table 17. The Average Number of Nuts per Candy Bar for Three Brands

Company	Mean Nuts/Bar
X	40
Y	40
Z	39.5

the companies provided on the mean number of nuts for each of the candy bars is summarized in Table 17.

The information looks very promising, but just to make sure the information is accurate, you decide to test the candy samples. You want to be certain Ellen will receive 40 nuts in each of the chocolate bars.

First, you test a bar from Company X. To your amazement, you discover 79 nuts in the first bar! So you test the remaining bars from Company X and obtain the results in Table 18.

Clearly, you cannot rely on Company X for 40 nuts per bar! You go on to test the samples from Company Y and obtain the results in Table 19.

These results are better than those for Company X, but they still will not satisfy Ellen. So on to

Table 18. The Number of Nuts in a Random Sample of Company X Candy Bars

Candy Bar	Number of Nuts
1	79
2	1
3	1
4	79
5	79
6	1

Table 19. The Number of Nuts in a Random
Sample of Company Y Candy Bars

Candy Bar	Number of Nuts
1	50
2	30
3	45
4	35
5	43
6	37

Company Z. Initially, this brand seemed the least promising of the three because the mean number of nuts per candy bar is 39.5, rather than 40. But as you can see in Table 20, the number of nuts in each of the Z chocolate bars is quite consistent, either 39 or 40 nuts per bar. The choice for Ellen's gift is clear: Brand Z.

Why were the means for brands X and Y so misleading? The mean gives you information about only the center of each distribution; it does not tell you about the spread of the data around the center, and it gives no indication as to the consistency of your data.

Table 20. The Number of Nuts in a Random
Sample of Company Z Candy Bars

Candy Bar	Number of Nuts
1	40
2	40
3	40
4	39
5	39
6	39

So an average taken by itself may not always be very meaningful. To completely understand the results of your experiments, you need a statistic describing the spread of the data.

There are several ways to measure the spread of data. The three most common statistics for the spread are the *range*, the *interquartile range*, and the *standard deviation*.

The range, sometimes called the *crude range*, is simply the difference between the maximum and minimum scores in your set of data.

$$range = maximum - minimum$$

The range for each of the candy companies is shown in Table 21.

The smaller the range, the smaller the spread of the scores. When the range is 0, there is no deviation or spread of scores around the mean. All the scores are exactly the same.

Unfortunately, the range gives no indication of whether the maximum or minimum value is an outlier or a score that is representative of your collected data. Furthermore, the range does not tell you whether there is only one score or 20 scores at the maximum or minimum value.

For this reason, the range is not the best estimate

Table 21. The Range of Nuts in a Random Sample of Three Candy Bars

Company	Max. – Min.	Range
X	79 – 1	78
Y	50 – 30	20
Z	40 – 39	1

of the spread of data, though it is a good quick estimate.

The interquartile range is more meaningful than the crude range. This statistic, commonly called the IQR, eliminates the data at the extremes, so that it is not skewed by outliers. It is the range of the half of the data at the center of the distribution. The IQR begins at the 25th percentile and ends at the 75th percentile.

Let's calculate the IQR for the 11 golf scores discussed previously:

$$81 \quad 83 \quad 86 \quad 87 \quad 88 \quad 89 \quad 90 \quad 91 \quad 95 \quad 102 \quad 105$$

The crude range is $105 - 81 = 24$. The total spread of the scores is 24 points. The quartiles for this group of data are as follows:

$$Q_1: 86 \qquad Q_2: 89 \qquad Q_3: 95$$

The IQR is calculated as follows:

$$
\begin{aligned}
IQR &= Q_3 - Q_1 \\
&= 95 - 86 \\
&= 9
\end{aligned}
$$

Thus, the middle half of the data has a spread of 9 points. There is a difference of only 9 points between the scores for the half of the team at the center of the distribution, whereas there is a difference of 24 points between the best and worst player. This indicates that the data clusters around the median.

The *standard deviation* is the most commonly used statistic for indicating the spread of data points. It gives a precise measure of how the scores are spread around the center, or the mean, of your data. The standard deviation takes into account the values of all the points rather than just a few key ones, as the IQR does. The following formula defines the standard deviation:

$$s = \sqrt{\frac{\Sigma(x - \bar{x})^2}{n - 1}}$$

where x is a data value, $\bar{x}$ is the mean, and n is the number of data points.

Let's compute the standard deviation for Brand Z, using the above formula. The values of x can be obtained from Table 20. The value of n is 6 and the value of $\bar{x}$ is 39.5. Substituting the values:

$$= \sqrt{\frac{(40 - 39.5)^2 + (40 - 39.5)^2 + (40 - 39.5)^2 + (39 - 39.5)^2 + (39 - 39.5)^2 + (39 - 39.5)^2}{5}}$$

$$s = \sqrt{\frac{0.5^2 + 0.5^2 + 0.5^2 + (-0.5)^2 + (-0.5)^2 + (-0.5)^2}{5}}$$

$$s = \sqrt{\frac{1.5}{5}}$$

$$s = \sqrt{0.3}$$

$$s = 0.55$$

Table 22 gives the standard deviation of the number of nuts for each of the three candy bars.

The lower the standard deviation, the less the data varies from the mean. As expected, brand Z is the most consistent in the number of nuts each bar contains. It has a standard deviation of 0.55. This

Table 22. Standard Deviations for Three Candy Bars	
Brand	**Standard Deviation**
X	42.72
Y	7.32
Z	0.55

means that the number of nuts in each candy bar is almost exactly the same, varying by only about half a nut.

Both X and Y have much larger standard deviations, indicating that the number of nuts varies a great deal. So the larger the value, the greater the spread of the scores around the mean—and the greater the range. A set of values that is totally consistent has a standard deviation of 0.

CHAPTER 4

THE NORMAL DISTRIBUTION

You are probably familiar with the expression "the teacher grades on a bell curve." You may know that in general, this bell-curve grading is a good thing for students taking difficult courses. With a bell curve, even if you get poor scores, you may end up with a good grade if you did better than most of the other students.

Now that you know a little statistics, you can get a better understanding of just what grading on a bell curve is. The bell curve refers to the shape of the frequency distribution of grades. If you graph the number of A's, B's, C's, D's, and F's given by a teacher who grades on a bell curve, you would get something that looks like a bell, as shown in Figure 9.

There are just a few A's and F's at the edges of the bell, but as you go in toward the middle, the num-

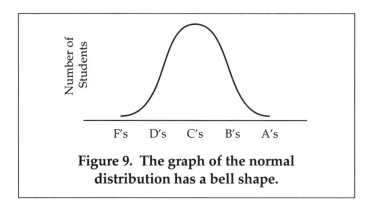

Figure 9. The graph of the normal distribution has a bell shape.

ber of B's and D's is higher, and the number of C's is the highest, at the top of the bell. The number of C's coincides with both the median and mean of the grades. Grades usually do not follow this ideal shape, but teachers who grade on a bell curve will adjust them to conform to it. Statisticians call this very special shape a *normal distribution*. Many large sets of data naturally follow a normal distribution.

Let's look at one example. The owner of Steve's Skaterama was interested in buying new skates for the women skaters, but he did not know how many of each size to order. So he surveyed the shoe sizes of his entire population of 340 women customers and used the results to create the frequency distribution in Table 23.

From this data, Steve concluded that the average

Some teachers grade tests on a curve. The "curve" is the plot of the normal distribution.

Table 23. Skating Shoe Sizes of 340 Women

Size	f
4	5
5	25
6	35
7	65
8	80
9	65
10	35
11	25
12	5

skating shoe size for his population was 8 with a standard deviation of 1.73. Since the shoes come in only full sizes, these two statistics tell Steve that most of the women wear sizes from 6 to 10. When Steve plotted the data, he obtained the frequency polygon in Figure 10.

He noticed that the curve was somewhat bell-shaped, had a single peak at the mean of 8, and was symmetric about this mean. In other words, it resembled a normal distribution.

To determine whether a distribution is truly normal, statisticians use a complex formula that includes the mean and standard deviation for a population. This formula can be found in any college-level statistics textbook. For the purposes of this book, we will examine the characteristics of the normal distribution, which are important for carrying out hypothesis testing in later chapters.

In every normal distribution, both the mean and the median are located in the center of the curve—at the top of the bell. In order to simplify calculations,

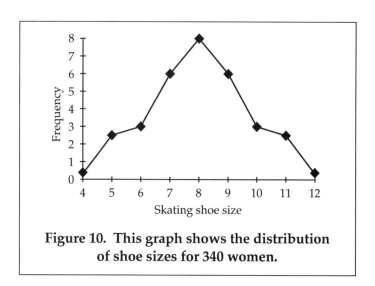

Figure 10. This graph shows the distribution of shoe sizes for 340 women.

statisticians have created a *standard normal curve,* in which the mean has been given a value of zero. Values to the left of the mean are negative and values to the

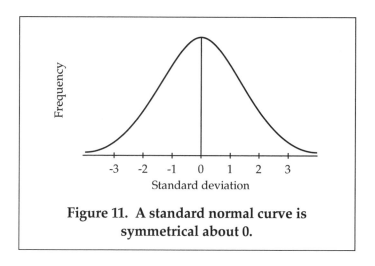

Figure 11. A standard normal curve is symmetrical about 0.

right are positive, as in Figure 11. Thus, the values are symmetrical around the mean.

What is more, the values along the horizontal axis of a standard normal curve correspond to units of standard deviation. As you recall from Chapter 3, the standard deviation is a measure of a curve's spread. In the standard normal curve, the standard deviation is given a value of 1.0. For a normal distribution, statisticians have determined that:

- Approximately 68% of the data values fall within one standard deviation of the mean.
- Approximately 95% of the data values fall within two standard deviations of the mean.
- Approximately 99% of the data values fall within three standard deviations of the mean.

These ideas may become clearer if you look at Figure 12.

Statisticians work frequently with normal distributions because many sets of data fall naturally into the shape of a normal distribution. The properties of the normal distribution allow them to make reliable predictions about the entire population from a small sample. For example, normal distributions can give the *probability* that a piece of data from a population falls within a certain range of values. This will become clearer by looking at a specific case.

Battery manufacturers are always working to increase the life of their batteries because customers want batteries that will last as long as possible. One manufacturer, Dependable Batteries, ran tests on a random sample of its products and found that the life of the batteries seemed to follow a normal distribution; the lifetimes were distributed along a bell curve, with a mean of 600 hours at the peak, as shown in Figure 13. If the standard deviation was 100 hours,

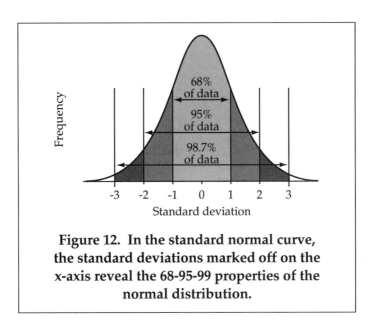

Figure 12. In the standard normal curve, the standard deviations marked off on the x-axis reveal the 68-95-99 properties of the normal distribution.

what is the probability that a battery selected at random will last from 600 to 700 hours?

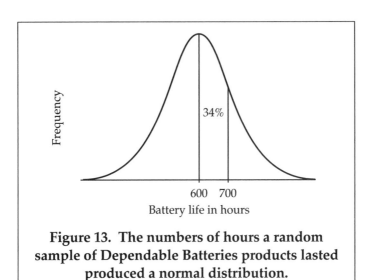

Figure 13. The numbers of hours a random sample of Dependable Batteries products lasted produced a normal distribution.

Since 700 is one standard deviation away from the mean, you know immediately that 34 percent of the batteries have lifetimes from 600 to 700 hours. Refer again to Figure 12 to verify this. Thus, there is a 34 percent chance that any battery picked at random from the assembly line will have a lifetime of 600 to 700 hours. Since a percentage of 100 gives a probability of 1.00, a percentage of 34% could be restated as a probability of 0.34.

CORRELATION

Correlation describes the relationship between two variables. A statistic called the *correlation coefficient*, indicates the strength of the relationship between two sets of data on a scale of 0 to 1, with 0 signifying that there is no relationship.

The correlation coefficient is different from the statistics you have studied so far because it applies to two sets of data rather than to a single distribution.

Let's look at a situation in which the correlation would be useful. Suppose you are interested in determining whether there is a relationship between midterm grades and final exam scores. In other words, you want to know whether students with good midterm grades scored well on their final exams, and whether those with poor midterm grades tended to score poorly on their finals. You select three science classes to study and choose a random sample of stu-

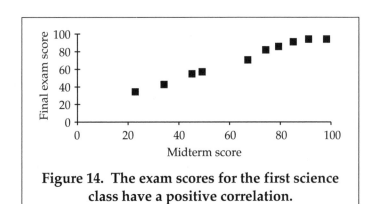

Figure 14. The exam scores for the first science class have a positive correlation.

dents from each class. The sample from the first class has the following grades:

Student	(1)	(2)	(3)	(4)	(5)	(6)	(7)	(8)	(9)	(10)
Midterm scores:	23	34	45	49	67	74	79	85	91	98
Final-exam scores:	35	43	55	57	71	82	86	91	94	95

Notice that there are a pair of scores for each of the ten students. If the midterm score for each student is plotted along the x-axis, and the final score along the y-axis, a relationship between the two types of grades may become apparent. Indeed, as shown in Figure 14, the graph reveals a linear relationship between the x and y values; the points approximate a straight line.

Since low values of x are paired with low values

Is there a correlation between students' midterm grades and their final exam scores?

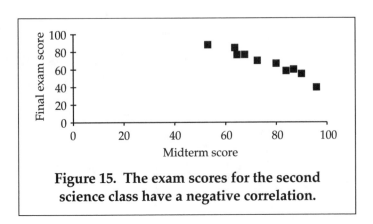

**Figure 15. The exam scores for the second
science class have a negative correlation.**

of y and high values of x are paired with high values
of y, the relationship is *positive*.

The second science class has the following scores:

Student	(1)	(2)	(3)	(4)	(5)	(6)	(7)	(8)	(9)	(10)
Midterm scores:	96	90	87	84	80	73	68	65	64	53
Final-exam scores:	40	55	60	59	67	70	77	78	85	90

When these scores are plotted, as in Figure 15,
you can see an inverse, or *negative*, linear relationship
between x and y variables. Students with high midterm
grades have low final grades and those with low
midterm grades have high final grades.

The scores from the third science class are as follows:

Student	(1)	(2)	(3)	(4)	(5)	(6)	(7)	(8)	(9)	(10)
Midterm scores:	23	75	35	64	94	86	45	54	46	99
Final-exam scores:	76	89	45	90	54	38	98	27	67	34

The graph of the data is shown in Figure 16. It is obvious that there is little or no linear correlation between x and y because the points seem to be scattered randomly.

In fact, Figures 14, 15, and 16 are called *scatter diagrams* because they let you see how the data values are scattered. This scatter is a measure of the correlation between the x and y values. Thus, scatter plots give a visual, intuitive feel for the value of the correlation coefficient.

The basic scatter diagram portrays the direction, form, and strength of any relationship between two variables. But it is not always easy to guess the degree of the relationship from a visual inspection of a scatter diagram. The interpretation of a scatter diagram is surprisingly subjective. Stretching or compressing the graph, for instance, can dramatically alter its appearance.

Fortunately, rather than relying solely on a scatter plot, you can calculate a value for the correlation. The correlation coefficient, r, is a value between -1 and 1. If there is no correlation at all, the value of r is 0.

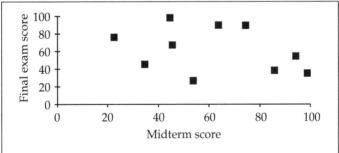

Figure 16. The exam scores for the third science class have no correlation.

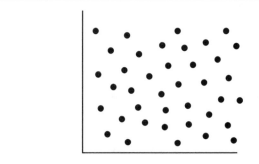

**Figure 17. This scatter plot shows data
with a correlation coefficient $r = 0$.**

Figure 17 shows what a scatter diagram for $r = 0$ might look like.

If $r = 1$ or $r = -1$, then there is a perfect linear relationship between x and y values. All the graphed points would lie exactly on a straight line. Figure 18 shows the scatter diagram for these cases.

If r is between 0 and 1, then the x and y values have a positive correlation, as shown in Figure 19.

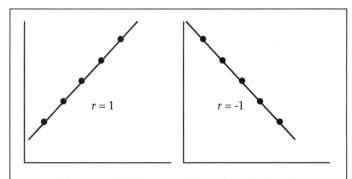

$r = 1$ $r = -1$

**Figure 18. These scatter plots indicate
correlation coefficients of $r = 1$ and $r = -1$.**

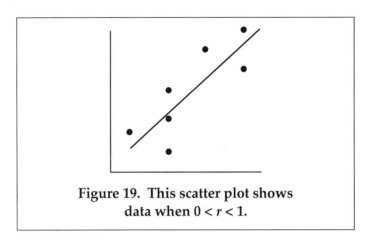

Figure 19. This scatter plot shows data when 0 < *r* < 1.

If *r* is between -1 and 0, then the *x* and *y* values have a negative correlation, as shown in Figure 20.

The sign of the correlation coefficient indicates the direction of the relationship. So both *r* = -0.07 and *r* = +0.07 indicate a relationship of exactly the same strength but in opposite directions. The formula for calculating the linear correlation coefficient is called the *Pearson r correlation coefficient formula*. This formu-

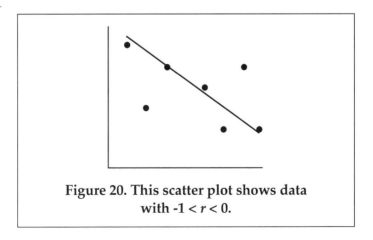

Figure 20. This scatter plot shows data with -1 < *r* < 0.

la may look overwhelming at first, but you will find that it is relatively simple to use.

Before calculating r, it is always a good idea to first draw a scatter diagram to get a rough idea of the correlation. The formula is:

$$r = \frac{\sum xy - \frac{1}{n}\sum x \sum y}{\sqrt{(\sum x^2 - \frac{(\sum x)^2}{n})(\sum y^2 - \frac{(\sum y)^2}{n})}}$$

The formula can get complicated with large amounts of data, but you can use a calculator or a computer program to simplify your task.

Let's look at the correlation between a child's height and age. The growth chart of Isabelle between the ages of 3 and $5^1/2$ years is as follows:

Age in years:	3.0	3.5	4.0	4.5	5.0	5.5
Height in feet:	2.9	3.1	3.2	3.4	3.4	3.5

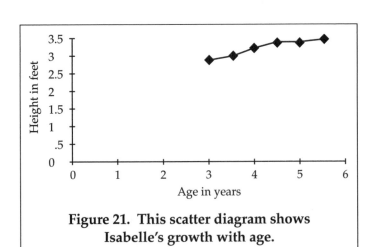

Figure 21. This scatter diagram shows Isabelle's growth with age.

Does Isabelle's height correlate with her age?

First, make a scatter diagram to determine whether the correlation seems positive, negative, or close to zero. Plot age along the x-axis and height along the y-axis, as shown in Figure 21.

Table 24. The Sums for Calculating the Correlation Coefficient

x (age)	y (height)	x^2	y^2	xy
3.0	2.9	9.0	8.41	8.70
3.5	3.1	12.25	9.61	10.85
4.0	3.2	16.00	10.24	12.80
4.5	3.4	20.25	11.56	15.30
5.0	3.4	25.00	11.56	17.00
5.5	3.5	30.25	12.25	19.25
sums:				
25.5	19.5	112.75	63.63	83.90

You should be able to easily see that the correlation is positive. Now to calculate r, you must first find the sums of x, y, x^2, y^2, and xy. You can obtain the values for $(\Sigma x)^2$ and $(\Sigma y)^2$ from Σx and Σy. The easiest way to determine all of these values is to create Table 24.

From the table, you can see that:

$$\Sigma x = 25.5$$
$$\Sigma y = 19.5$$
$$\Sigma x^2 = 112.75$$
$$\Sigma y^2 = 63.63$$
$$\Sigma xy = 83.90$$
$$(\Sigma x)^2 = 650.25$$
$$(\Sigma y)^2 = 380.25$$

Next, substitute these values in the Pearson r correlation coefficient formula:

$$r = \frac{\Sigma xy - \frac{1}{n}\Sigma x \, \Sigma y}{\sqrt{(\Sigma x^2 - \frac{(\Sigma x)^2}{n})(\Sigma y^2 - \frac{(\Sigma y)^2}{n})}}$$

$$r = \frac{(83.90) - (\frac{1}{6})(25.25)(19.5)}{\sqrt{(112.75 - \frac{650.25}{6})(63.63 - \frac{380.25}{6})}}$$

$$r = \frac{83.90 - 82.88}{\sqrt{(112.75 - 108.38)(63.63 - 63.63)}}$$

$$r = \frac{1.02}{\sqrt{(4.37)(.25)}}$$

$$r = \frac{1.02}{\sqrt{1.09}}$$

$$r = \frac{1.02}{1.04}$$

$$r = 0.98$$

A correlation coefficient of 0.98 means that there is a very high positive correlation between Isabelle's age and growth.

When using this formula, it is important to remember that the Pearson r correlation coefficient reflects only the *linear* relationship between two variables. If you calculate a low correlation coefficient, you cannot immediately conclude that there is little or no relationship between the two variables you are studying. They could be related in a nonlinear way. This is much more difficult to test for and beyond the scope of this book. Just remember that the failure to find a correlation means one of two things:

1. The variables are unrelated.
2. The variables are related in a nonlinear fashion.

If you do find a correlation, it is also important to avoid assuming that a change in one variable is causing a change in the other variable. A strong correlation does not necessarily imply cause-and-effect. Some other known or unknown variable could be causing changes in both variables.

INFERENTIAL STATISTICS

The preceding chapters deal with statistics that apply to a sample taken from a population. In the real world, it is not enough to work with samples. Scientists must draw conclusions about the entire population based on what they learn from samples. In this chapter, you will learn techniques for making inferences about the population from samples.

To avoid confusion, statisticians identify the measurable characteristics, or statistics, of a sample with regular lowercase letters and the statistics for a population with lowercase Greek letters. For example, the symbol for the mean of a sample is $\bar{x}$, whereas the symbol for the mean of a population is the Greek letter mu, μ, which is pronounced "moo." The symbol for the standard deviation of a sample is s, and the symbol for the standard deviation of a population is the Greek letter sigma, or σ, which is pronounced "sigma." The symbol for the correlation coefficient for a sample is r, whereas the symbol for the population correlation coefficient is the Greek letter rho, or ρ, which is pronounced "row."

HYPOTHESIS TESTING

If a statistician asks 100 people how they intend to vote in an upcoming election, his primary goal is not to determine exactly how these 100 people will vote, but to infer from this sample how the entire voting population will cast their ballots.

Hypothesis testing is a mathematical procedure for analyzing the statistics from a sample in order to make inferences about the population. As you learned in the introduction, a hypothesis is a guess, or conjecture, about a population parameter that you make before you begin an experiment. Whether you accept or reject the hypothesis will depend on the information you acquire from studying the sample.

Hypothesis testing is a statistical procedure that enables you to decide to accept or reject your original hypothesis. This is accomplished by restating the original hypothesis in the form of two mutually exclusive hypotheses; the *null hypothesis* and the *alternative hypothesis*.

In a null hypothesis, the researcher proposes that there is no difference between the sample statistic and the population parameter. The symbol for the null hypothesis is H_o. Mathematically, the null hypothesis always tests the sample statistic value against the population parameter; that is, $\bar{x}$, the value for the mean obtained from the sample, is tested against μ for the population, and, r, the correlation coefficient for the sample is tested against the ρ for the population.

In an alternative hypothesis, the researcher proposes that there is a difference between the sample statistic and the population parameter. The symbol for the alternative hypothesis is H_1.

A statistician works with both the null and alternative hypothesis at the same time. Suppose you want to see if there is a difference between two manufacturing methods. First, you create the null hypothesis. You proclaim that there *is no difference* between the two manufacturing methods; that is, both methods give exactly the same results. Second, you create the alternative hypothesis. You proclaim that there *is a difference* between the two manufacturing methods; both methods do not give the same results. In other words, one manufacturing method is clearly different from the other.

The null hypothesis is created just to see if you can reject it. It might seem odd, but statisticians discuss the results of hypothesis testing only in terms of the null hypothesis; that is, they either reject or accept the null hypothesis. Statisticians never use the alternative hypothesis to discuss the results of hypothesis testing. In the example on the two manufacturing methods, if you discover that there *is no difference* between the two manufacturing methods, you would accept the null hypothesis. If you discover that there *is a difference* between the two manufacturing methods, you would reject the null hypothesis.

For a more complex example, suppose a teacher gives her twelfth-grade class a final examination and the average score is 75. In other words, her sample of 36 students has a mean score of $\bar{x} = 75$. From her years of experience teaching the class, the teacher knows that the average score for all students who have taken the test is a μ of 68, with a standard deviation, σ, of 6. She wants to know whether this year's class is really superior to previous classes, as the numbers seem to indicate.

It may seem obvious to you that this year's average is superior to the average from previous years. But if the test scores in the population varied quite a bit, a difference of 7 points in the average score may be insignificant from a statistical point of view. Hypothesis testing can be used to determine whether the 7 point difference between a sample mean of 75 and a population mean of 68 is meaningful, or *statistically significant*.

The null hypothesis, H_o, is stated as follows:

$$H_o: \mu = 68$$

This is a mathematical way of saying there is no difference between the population mean of 68 and the sample mean of 75. In other words, a group of 36 students who scored a mean of 75 could have come from the population of previous students.

The alternative hypothesis, H_1, is as follows:

$$H_1: \mu > 68$$

This is a mathematical way of saying there is a difference between the population mean of 68 and the sample mean of 75. It says that the class is representative of a population with a mean greater than 68. In other words, a group of 36 students who scored a mean of 75 could not possibly have come from the population of previous students; they must be from a different, superior population.

It is important to keep in mind that any decisions you make based on samples always have the possibility of being in error. If you reject the null hypothesis when it is in fact true, you have made an error

[86]

Table 25. Possible Outcomes of Hypothesis Testing

Truth about the population

Decision	H_o True	H_o False
Reject H_o	Type I Error	Correct Decision No Error
Accept H_o	Correct Decision No Error	Type II Error

known as a *type I error*. On the other hand, if you accept the null hypothesis when it is in fact false, you have made an error known as a *type II error*. Table 25 outlines all possible outcomes of hypothesis testing.

The probability of a type I error is called the *level of significance* of a test and is denoted by the Greek letter α (alpha). Scientists choose the level of significance before they have collected any data so as not to influence their results. It is a measure of the risk they are willing to take of getting a type I error. The lower you set the level of significance, the less the likelihood of a type I error, but the greater the likelihood of a type II error.

One of the most commonly used values for alpha is 0.05. If you choose alpha to be 0.05, then you are requiring the hypothesis test to give you a 5% *level of significance*. This means that there are only five chances out of 100 that the null hypothesis will be rejected when it should be accepted.

Another commonly used value for alpha is $\alpha = 0.01$. A 1% level of significance indicates that the null hypothesis will be rejected when it should be accepted only once in 100 cases.

Let's return to the example in which this year's students obtained an average of 75 on the final exam.

Suppose that the teacher has chosen a level of significance of 5%. The next step is to test the hypothesis.

Since you know both the mean and the standard deviation for the population, the proper statistical test to use in this case is the z *test*. The formula for the z test is:

$$z = \frac{\bar{x} - \mu}{\dfrac{\sigma}{\sqrt{n}}}$$

The formula may seem complicated at first, but you have all the values needed to calculate z. You know:

- $\bar{x} = 75$; the sample mean, this year's final exam average, is 75.
- $\mu = 68$; the population mean, the average for all the previous years, is 68.
- $\sigma = 6$; the population standard deviation is 6.
- $n = 36$; the sample size, the number of students in the present class, is 36.

Substituting these values into the z test formula, you obtain:

$$z = \frac{\bar{x} - \mu}{\dfrac{\sigma}{\sqrt{n}}}$$

$$z = \frac{75 - 68}{\dfrac{6}{\sqrt{36}}}$$

$$z = 7$$

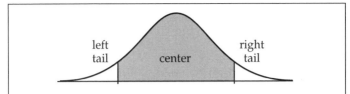

Figure 22. The standard normal curve is divided into three sections for hypothesis testing.

You have calculated a value of $z = 7$, but what does this mean? Should you accept or reject the null hypothesis? In order to interpret z values, statisticians use as a geometric model the standard normal curve, which was explained in Chapter 4. Remember, the standard normal curve is symmetrical, and has a value of 0 for the mean. The values along the horizontal axis of the normal curve correspond to z values.

The standard normal curve consists of a left tail, the center, and a right tail, as shown in Figure 22.

For the purposes of hypothesis testing, the area in the tails is known as the rejection region. The remaining area is known as the acceptance region. The value on the horizontal axis that separates the rejection region from the acceptance region is known as the *critical value*. You will reject the null hypothesis if the z value falls in the rejection region and you will accept the null hypothesis if the z value falls in the acceptance region of the standard normal curve model. See Figure 23.

A list of critical values for different levels of significance (α) can be found in Table I in Appendix C. For our example, the rejection region is in the right tail only since we want to know whether the population mean for this year's class is *greater than* the mean for previous classes. So we must look up the value for

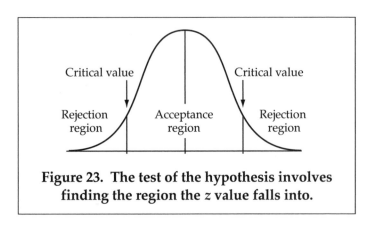

Figure 23. The test of the hypothesis involves finding the region the z value falls into.

a one-tailed test. (Two-tailed tests will be explained later). The critical value for this example, where $\alpha =$ 0.05, is 1.65. This means that the value 1.65 will separate the rejection region from the acceptance region as shown in Figure 24.

Since the value you obtained from the z formula, $z = 7.00$, is larger than 1.65, your z value falls in the rejection region, as shown in Figure 25.

Therefore, you reject the null hypothesis. That

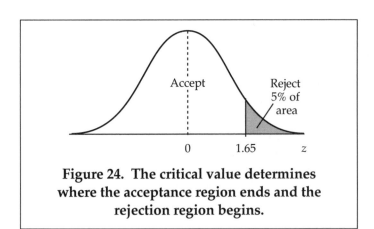

Figure 24. The critical value determines where the acceptance region ends and the rejection region begins.

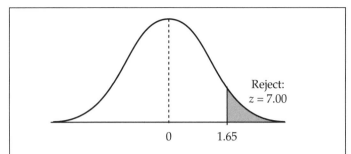

Figure 25. The z value clearly falls in the rejection region, so you must reject the null hypothesis.

means you reject the idea that this class is from the same population as all previous classes that have taken the final exam.

LET THERE BE LIGHT

The Superlight Lightbulb Company claims that the 100-watt bulb it sells has an average bulb life of $\mu = 1{,}000$ hours with a standard deviation of $\sigma = 75$ hours. Suppose you wanted to confirm this by conducting an experiment on a random sample of 64 bulbs. After leaving the bulbs on until they burn out, you find that the average bulb life for the sample is $\bar{x} = 975$ hours. Have you caught the company in a lie? Is the real mean less than 1,000 hours?

Our null hypothesis is

$$H_o: \mu = 1{,}000$$

which says that there is no significant difference between the average bulb life of the sample and the average bulb life of the population, as specified by the company.

The alternative hypothesis is:

$$H_1: \mu < 1{,}000$$

which says that the average bulb life of the sample is less than the average bulb life of the population.

Let's assume that the Superlight Lightbulb Company has agreed to accept our findings, at an $\alpha = 0.01$ level of significance. Since you know both the population mean and population standard deviation, you can use the z test.

Before finding the z value, let's get the critical value from Table I in Appendix C. It is a good idea to first sketch your distribution with acceptance and rejection regions marked so that you do not get confused in the course of the z test. The geometric model of the problem is shown in Figure 26.

In Table I, you will find a z value of 2.33 for a 0.01 level of significance. You must add a negative sign to this value because the average life of the sample bulbs ($\bar{x} = 975$) is less than the average life of the population bulbs ($\mu = 1{,}000$). You want to know whether the population mean for this sample is actually *less than* 1,000

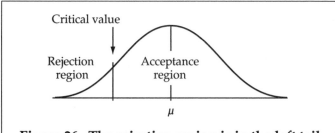

Figure 26. The rejection region is in the left tail because the life of your lightbulbs is less than the company's average.

hours. So you must use the left tail, or negative tail, to test your null hypothesis. The z test says to reject H_o if $z < -2.33$. You can now calculate the value of z for the lightbulbs:

$$z = \frac{\bar{x} - \mu}{\dfrac{\alpha}{\sqrt{n}}}$$

$$z = \frac{1000 - 975}{\dfrac{75}{\sqrt{64}}}$$

$$z = -2.67$$

Now you have all the information you need to draw a conclusion. The value of $z = -2.67$ falls in the rejection region. You must reject H_o and conclude that the mean of the bulbs is not as the manufacturer states, but is less than 1,000 hours. Superlight will have to change its advertising claim.

In some cases, you will not know both the population mean and the population standard deviation. If you know the population mean, but not the population standard deviation, then you should use the t test rather than the z test. The next example illustrates how to use the t test.

SIZING UP FISH WITH THE T-TEST

Tara owns a private fishing pond. She boasts that the average length of fish in the pond is 15 inches ($\mu = 15$). To see whether she is telling the truth, you catch a sample of 23 fish from various random locations in the pond. You find the average length of this sample

Do Tara's fish really average 15 inches in length?

of fish to have a sample mean of 10.7 inches ($\bar{x} = 10.7$) with a sample standard deviation, $s = 4.8$ inches. Given this data, can Tara's claim possibly be true? Could this sample have come from a population whose mean is 15, or are the fish shorter than she states? Find the answer using a level of significance of $\alpha = 0.01$.

The null hypothesis is:

$$H_o: \mu = 15$$

The alternative hypothesis is:

$$H_1: \mu < 15$$

The null hypothesis says that the average size of the fish in the pond is less than 15 inches. Here again, we must carry out a one-tailed test.

In this case, you cannot use the z test because you do not know the population standard deviation. The t *test* is a good test to use in this situation. The t test requires that you know the sample mean, the sample standard deviation, and the population mean. The underlying distribution, known as the *student's t distribution*, is suitable for relatively small samples. As the sample size increases to about 200, the t distribution approaches the shape of the normal distribution. As shown in Figure 27, the t distribution has thicker tails than the standard normal distribution.

The figure shows that the shape of the student's t distribution depends on the sample size. The sample size determines the *degrees of freedom* of the t distribution. This parameter, represented by df, is equal to the sample size minus 1:

$$df = n - 1 = 23 - 1 = 22$$

There are 22 degrees of freedom in this sample.

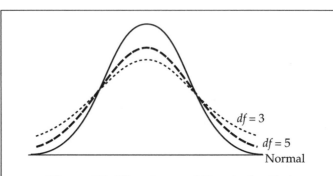

Figure 27. The shape of the student's *t* distribution depends on the number of degrees of freedom.

You will be calculating a *t* value for your problem, just as you calculated a *z* value in the previous example. Before finding the *t* value, sketch your distribution, marking acceptance and rejection regions. As in the lightbulb problem, the rejection region will be in the left tail since we want to know whether the mean is less than the stated value. The geometric model for this problem is shown in Figure 28.

Next, determine the critical value of *t* for this problem in Table II in Appendix C. Notice that Table

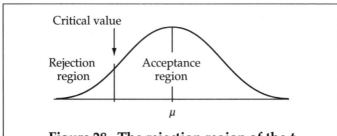

Figure 28. The rejection region of the *t* distribution is in the left tail because the fish you measured were shorter than Tara's claim.

II is quite different from Table I. In Table I, you need to know only the level of significance, but in Table II, you need to know α and the degrees of freedom for your problem.

For $\alpha = 0.01$ and 22 degrees of freedom, you should get a critical value of -2.51 from Table II. Notice that, as in the lightbulb example, the value must be made negative. That is because you are testing whether the average length of the sample of fish is less than the average length of the population of fish. So the t test says to reject H_o if $t < -2.51$, as shown in Figure 29.

The formula for t is:

$$t = \frac{\bar{x} - \mu}{\dfrac{s}{\sqrt{n}}}$$

$$t = \frac{10.7 - 15}{\dfrac{4.8}{\sqrt{23}}} = -4.3$$

Since $t = -4.3$ falls in the rejection region, you must reject the null hypothesis, and conclude that the fish are smaller than Tara claimed.

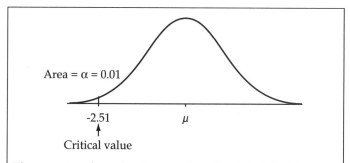

Figure 29. The rejection region for this t test is very small because the level of significance is only 0.01.

TAILS OF TWO REGIONS

The examples you have worked so far involve one rejection region located in one tail of the distribution. As a result, the hypothesis tests you performed are called *one-tailed tests*. A *two-tailed test* is necessary when the alternative hypothesis contains the not-equal sign (≠), instead of a greater-than or less-than symbol.

Such a situation would occur, for instance, in the testing of jeans for consistency in size. A jeans manufacturer wants to make sure that the average waist measurement of its size 32-inch jeans be within 1/2-inch of the labeled size. When a random sample of the jeans are inspected for quality, the manufacturer is interested only in whether the average size of the sample is significantly different from 32 inches. It does not matter whether the jeans are too big or too small; they will be rejected in either case. In this situation, the two hypotheses would be:

$$H_o: \mu = 32$$
$$H_1: \mu \neq 32$$

The geometric model for such a situation would look like Figure 30.

Thus, if the z or t value falls in either of the two tail regions, the null hypothesis must be rejected. Mathematically speaking, you would compare the absolute values of the test values as follows:

Reject H_o if $|$ calculated $z| > |z$ test value $|$

The brackets designate absolute value, which is the value of a number excluding any negative sign.

It should be clear to you by now that the null hypothesis always contains an equal sign because you

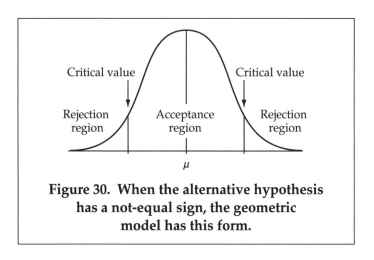

Critical value

Critical value

Rejection region

Acceptance region

Rejection region

μ

Figure 30. When the alternative hypothesis has a not-equal sign, the geometric model has this form.

are testing for no significant difference between the sample mean and the population mean. In making the hypothesis, you are assuming that the sample has come from the population. The alternative hypothesis, however, always contains one of three mathematical symbols: $>$, $<$, or $\neq$. As shown in Table 26, if the symbol is $>$, then the rejection region is in the right tail; if it is $<$, the rejection region is in the left tail; and if it is $\neq$, then the rejection region is in both tails.

Table 26. Determining Rejection Regions

If the symbol in the alternative hypothesis is	One Tail $<$	Two Tail $\neq$	One Tail $>$
then the critical or rejection region consists of	one region on the left side	two regions, one on each side	one region on the right side

THE ρ-TEST

If your underlying distribution is the normal distribution and you want to test whether the correlation coefficient that you have obtained from your sample comes from a population in which the correlation coefficient is 0, you can apply the ρ-test. Remember from Chapter 5 that a correlation coefficient of 0 means that there is *no* relationship between the two variables.

For instance, suppose your friend Leo says he thinks there is a strong correlation between the amount of natural gas used to heat his home and the number of degree-days for the 9 months shown in Table 27. (A measure of the severity of the weather, a degree-day is registered for every degree the temperature falls below 65°F per day). Using the data in Table 27, Leo found a sample correlation coefficient of $r = 0.989$, which is a very strong relationship.

You want to know whether Leo's finding was just a fluke or whether there is indeed a correlation between gas consumption and degree days. In other words, is it possible that Leo's sample correlation could have come from a population in which the true correlation is zero?

This question leads to the following null hypothesis:

$$H_o: \rho = 0$$

Table 27. Leo's Gas Usage for 9 Months

Month	Oct.	Nov.	Dec.	Jan.	Feb.	Mar.	Apr.	May	June
Degree Days	15.6	26.8	37.8	36.4	35.5	18.6	15.3	7.9	0
Gas Usage	5.2	6.1	8.7	8.5	8.8	4.9	4.5	2.5	1.1

where ρ is the correlation coefficient for the population from which this sample was drawn.

Since Leo expects gas consumption to be positively related to degree-days, it is appropriate to test the above null hypothesis against the following one-tailed alternative hypothesis:

$$H_1: \rho > 0$$

To test the null hypothesis, you must use the ρ test, which is a special form of the t test. The underlying distribution of the ρ test is the student's t distribution. For the ρ test, you must calculate a value for t using a different equation from the one used for the t test. Use the following formula for t when you want to test whether a population correlation coefficient is 0 (i.e. $H_o: \rho = 0$):

$$t = \frac{r\sqrt{n-2}}{\sqrt{1-r^2}}$$

where n is the number of pairs of data values, which in our case is 9.

For the ρ test, the number of degrees of freedom is the number of data values minus 2, as follows:

$$df = n - 2$$
$$df = 9 - 2$$
$$df = 7$$

Suppose you select a level of significance of 0.01. Now you can draw the geometric model for the test as shown in Figure 31.

Because the alternative hypothesis has a greater-than sign, you have a one-tailed test with one rejection region as shown in the diagram. Now you must determine the critical value using Table II in Appendix

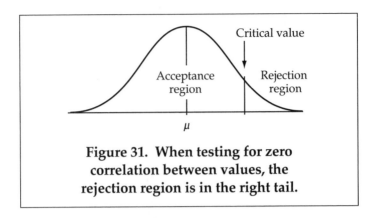

Figure 31. When testing for zero correlation between values, the rejection region is in the right tail.

C. Looking in the row for $df = 7$, you should find a critical value of 3.0.

Calculating the t test statistic, you should get:

$$t = \frac{.989 \sqrt{9-2}}{\sqrt{1-.989^2}}$$

$$t = \frac{26166}{.1479}$$

$$t = 17.69$$

Clearly, you can reject the null hypothesis, H_o, since $17.7 > 3.0$. Now Leo has strong evidence that gas consumption is positively related to degree-days.

OTHER TESTS

There are many tests other than the z, t, and p tests that can be used in hypothesis testing. Each one is designed for a specific type of distribution and set of circumstances. Now, let's look at examples using another of the more commonly used tests: the chi-square test. Chi is the Greek symbol χ, pronounced "kī."

Suppose you are interested in the number of baseball games that were played in each of the World Series between 1922 to 1965. Since the first team to win 4 games wins the series, the World Series can last anywhere from 4 to 7 games. The number of games played per series for the period from 1922 to 1965 is shown in Table 28.

The series went to 4 games in 9 years, to 5 games in 8 years, and so on. The most frequently played number was 7 games, which happened in a whopping 18 years. The data seems to indicate that it is more likely that 7 games will be played than any other number. But is this true? Or is it equally likely that any number of games will be played?

This is a different kind of statistical question from the examples discussed previously. Up until now, you have worked with single statistics, either the mean or the correlation coefficient. However, in this example you are interested in comparing the distribution of data from sample years against a theoretical distribution in which each piece of data has the same probability of occurring. The chi-square test answers the following question: "How well does the observed distribution fit the theoretical distribution?"

Table 28. Number of World Series Games (1922–1965)

Number of games in the World Series	4	5	6	7
Frequency of occurrence f_o between 1922 and 1965	9	8	9	18

The formula for the chi-square statistic is:

$$\chi^2 = \Sigma \frac{(f_o - f_e)^2}{f_e}$$

where f_o is the symbol for the actual, or observed, frequency count and f_e is the symbol for the expected frequency count.

The null hypothesis states that each event is equally likely to occur. This means that you expect the World Series to last for 4, 5, 6, or 7 games an equal number of times. This expected frequency can be calculated by finding the mean of the number of games played in each World Series from 1922 to 1965, as follows:

$$f_e = (9 + 8 + 9 + 18)/4$$
$$= 44/4$$
$$= 11$$

The null hypothesis states that each event is equally likely to occur. In other words, the World Series will last 4, 5, 6, and 7 games an equal number of times. Therefore:

$$H_o: f_e = 11$$

The alternative hypothesis states that each event is not equally likely to occur. In other words, the World Series will not last 4, 5, 6, and 7 games an equal number of times. Therefore:

$$H_1: f_e \neq 11$$

Let's test these hypotheses with a level of significance, $\alpha = 0.05$. The chi-square distribution is shown

The Pirates win the 1960 World Series in Game 7. Is it more likely for the World Series to go to seven games than any other number?

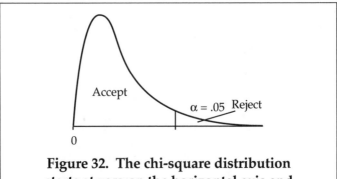

Figure 32. The chi-square distribution starts at zero on the horizontal axis and rises in the positive direction.

in Figure 32 with the rejection region marked. This is the geometric model for the problem.

Notice that the chi-square values—the values along the horizontal axis—are always positive and that only one rejection region is possible, in the single tail of the distribution. For $\alpha = 0.05$, the rejection region makes up 5% of the area under the curve.

The shape of the chi-square distribution depends on the number of distinct values in the problem, or more specifically, the number of degrees of freedom, df. As in the t test, df is equal to the number of different categories, k, minus 1. In this case:

$$df = k - 1$$
$$df = 4 - 1$$
$$df = 3$$

You can now look up the chi-square test value in Table III in Appendix C, which is set up in the same way as Table II for the t distributions. For an alpha value of 0.05, the critical value is 7.82. Thus, your test decision will be to reject H_0 if $\chi^2 \geq 7.82$.

Now you can calculate the chi-square value for this problem:

$$\chi^2 = \Sigma \frac{(f_o - f_e)^2}{f_e}$$

$$\chi^2 = \Sigma \frac{(9 - 11)^2}{11} + \frac{(8 - 11)^2}{11} + \frac{(9 - 11)^2}{11} + \frac{(18 - 11)^2}{11}$$

$$\chi^2 = \Sigma \frac{(-2)^2}{11} + \frac{(-3)^2}{11} + \frac{(-2)^2}{11} + \frac{(7)^2}{11}$$

$$\chi^2 = \frac{66}{11} = 6$$

Since a χ^2 value of 6 is less than 7.82, you must accept the null hypothesis. That means it is equally likely to have 4, 5, 6, or 7 games in a World Series.

GENERAL GUIDELINES FOR HYPOTHESIS TESTING

One of the most difficult judgments you have to make in hypothesis testing is which statistical test to use for your given data. The following guidelines will help you make your decision.

THE Z TEST
Use this test when:
- You know the mean and standard deviation for the population you are testing against.
- The underlying distribution is the normal curve. This is usually true for large populations.

Look up critical values for the z test in Table I in Appendix C. To calculate z:

$$z = \frac{\bar{x} - \mu}{\dfrac{\sigma}{\sqrt{n}}}$$

THE T TEST
Use this test when:
- You know only the mean for the population you want to test your sample against, as well as the sample mean and sample standard deviation.
- The underlying distribution is the student's t distribution, a family of curves that vary according to the number of degrees of freedom—a statistic related to the size of the sample. This distribution is accurate for small sample sizes—less than about 200 items.

Look up critical values for the t test in Table II in Appendix C using $df = n - 1$. To calculate t:

$$t = \frac{\bar{x} - \mu}{\dfrac{s}{\sqrt{n}}}$$

THE RHO TEST
Use this test when:
- The sample correlation coefficient, r, is known.
- You want to know whether your sample comes from a population in which the correlation coefficient is 0.

Look up the critical value for the test in Table II in Appendix C, using $df = n - 2$.

The formula for the ρ test is:

$$t = \frac{r \sqrt{n-2}}{\sqrt{1-r^2}}$$

THE CHI-SQUARE TEST
Use this test when:
- You want to know how well the observed distribution fits a theoretical distribution.

Look up critical values for the chi-square test in Table III in Appendix C. To calculate χ^2:

$$\chi^2 = \sum \frac{(f_o - f_e)^2}{f_e}$$

THE METHOD
A good practice in any hypothesis testing is to follow these general steps:

1. Summarize the known facts.
2. Establish the null hypothesis.
3. Establish the alternative hypothesis.
4. Choose the level of significance.
5. Choose the appropriate test statistic (z, t, χ^2, or ρ) for your problem.
6. Create a geometric model of your distribution.
7. Identify the critical value and the critical region.
8. Calculate the value of the test statistic.
9. Formulate a conclusion.

SCIENCE PROJECTS YOU CAN DO

Now that you have read about statistics and statistical testing methods, you can try out what you have learned on one or more of the following projects, or, of course, on a project of your own design.

For every project, you can use the statistical methods in this book to:

- Create a table or chart.
- Create a frequency distribution.
- Create a graph.
- Find the average.
- Find the standard deviation.
- Calculate percentiles.

In addition, after each project experiment is a series of questions that you can answer using hypothesis testing methods. Each project is just a starting

[110]

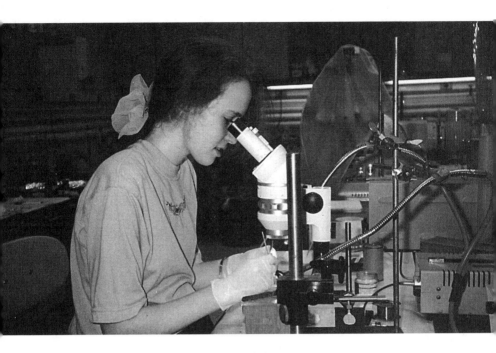

**A student conducts an experiment
on the luminescence of fireflies.**

point. There are many other questions you can answer
and experiments you can try in each of the areas. Use
your imagination and enjoy science!

1. Design an experiment to determine changes in the
humidity of air. You can do this by creating a hygrom-
eter, an instrument that measures humidity. Test the
effects of humidity on strands of silk thread, cotton
thread, and wool.

Use hypothesis testing to answer the following
questions:

- Is there a difference in hygroscopic action between
  the cotton and silk threads?

- Is there a difference in hygroscopic action between the cotton and wool threads? Between the silk and wool threads?

2. Design an experiment to determine the effects that enzymes found in detergents have on protein molecules. Hard-boiled eggs are one good source of protein molecules.

Use hypothesis testing to answer the following questions:

- Does the concentration of laundry detergent affect the results? Try different amounts of detergent

such as 1 teaspoon, 1 tablespoon, 3 tablespoons, and so on.
- How do different laundry detergents compare in their ability to clean stains from cloth?

3. Design an experiment to determine whether adding nutrients to seeds speeds their germination. Standard fertilizers are a good source of added nutrients.
Use hypothesis testing to answer the following questions:
- Is there a difference in germination speed if you use different commercial fertilizer products?
- Is there a difference in speed of germination if the seeds are planted in different types of soils?
- Do different types of seeds (grass seed, beans) germinate at different speeds?

4. Design an experiment to determine how water affects seed germination.
Use hypothesis testing to answer the following questions:
- Does temperature have an effect on germination?
- Does light have an effect on germination?
- Does planting depth have an effect on germination?

5. Design an experiment to determine whether some soils erode faster than others.
Use hypothesis testing to answer the following questions:
- Does the speed of watering (the daily amount of rainfall) affect the speed of soil erosion in different soils?
- Does the watering time (how long the rainfall lasts) affect the speed of soil erosion in different soils?

- Does the slope of the land affect the speed of soil erosion?

6. Design an experiment to determine whether vinegar is necessary for dyeing eggshells.
   Use hypothesis testing to answer the following questions:
   - Is the intensity of the color of the egg affected by the concentration of vinegar in the dye solution?
   - Does the temperature of the solution affect the results?
   - Does the color of the dye affect the results?

7. Design an experiment to see whether plants can be grown without soil in a nutrient solution, that is, using hydroponics.
   Use hypothesis testing to answer the following questions:
   - Does the amount of sunlight received by the plants affect their growth?
   - Does the amount of oxygen received by the plants affect their growth?
   - Does the growing medium affect the growth of hydroponically grown plants?

8. Design an experiment to test the viscosity of a liquid, such as water. You can do this by building a viscometer, an instrument that measures the flow rate of liquids.
   Use hypothesis testing to answer the following questions:
   - Does the temperature of the water affect its viscosity?
   - How does the viscosity of other liquids compare with the viscosity of water? Try liquids such as syrup, oil, dishwashing liquid, and so on.

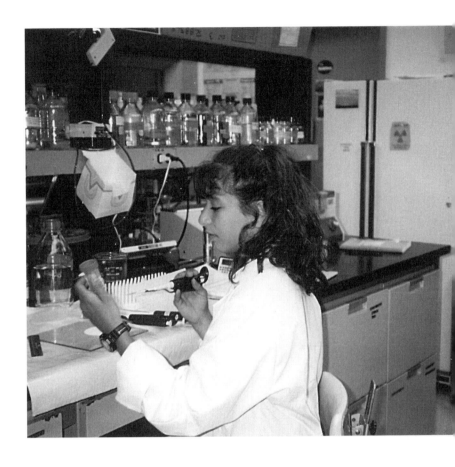

- Does the viscosity of a liquid affect its stickiness?
- Does temperature affect the viscosity of the different liquids?

9. Design an experiment to grow sucrose crystals in a gelatin solution.

Use hypothesis testing to answer the following questions:

- Does temperature affect crystal formation? Is there a difference in the sugar crystal formation if the solution is cooled at a slower rate by insulating the jar?

- Does evaporation rate affect crystal formation? Place the gelatin mixture in containers with different surface areas for evaporation.
- Does purity of solution affect crystal formation? Mix several types of sugar together in the gelatin solution.

10. Design an experiment to demonstrate the transportation of liquid through a plant's vascular system.

Use hypothesis testing to answer the following questions:

- Does the presence of leaves on a stem affect the rate of translocation?
- How does humidity affect the rate of transpiration?
- Does the amount of light affect the rate of translocation?
- Does the amount of light affect the rate of transpiration?

SCIENCE PROJECTS USING STATISTICS

Statistics is not just a mathematical exercise. It helps produce conclusions on some very important real-world issues. To give you an idea of the kinds of problems they have helped solve, a list of projects that high school students have done using the methods explained in this book is provided on the following pages. These were independent research projects submitted to science fair competitions. The description of each project is the abstract of the write-up submitted by the student.

A Study of the Possible Relationship Between Grade-Point Average, Gender, and Logic Testing Technique and Ability

A mathematical logic problem and its solution (Emmet 1972) was given to high school students. Nothing regarding the presence of the solution set was explained to the students. It was found that women viewed the solution sets as verification. Men viewed them as answers to be copied.

The Effects of the Algae Codium Fragile Used as a Fertilizer on the Growth of Plants: a Two-Year Study

The algae Codium Fragile was used as a plant fertilizer on fava beans and corn. The Codium Fragile was prepared in two different ways: (1) dried powder form, (2) boiling and then dissolving in solution. Ortho House Plant Food was used on a third group as a control. A fourth group received no fertilizer at all. It was found that there was no difference between the Codium Fragile (either dried or boiled) and the Ortho House Plant Food.

Phonological Revision Strategies in Young Children

This study examined the way that children make phonological repairs on their language when they perceive that they are not understood by their adult listener.

Is *Bacillus thurengensis israelensis* a Threat to Crustaceans such as *Artemia salina*?

This study investigated the effects of *Bacillus thurengensis israelensis* on *Artemia salina*. The study was based on the hypothesis that *Bti* is not harmful to *Artemia*

Dr. Eugene Katz, dean of biological sciences at the University at Stony Brook in New York, assists a student with her project.

salina regardless of concentration. *Artemia salina* were exposed to *Bti* concentrations of 0.01, 0.10 and 1.00 grams per 3 liters. Through statistical analysis it was shown that those *Artemia salina* exposed to the lower concentrations were unaffected, whereas those exposed to the higher concentrations experienced significantly higher mortality rates.

An Analysis of Ball Clay Pipe Fragments from the Terry-Mulford Site, Orient, New York

This project was an analysis of the ball clay pipe fragments recovered from the Terry-Mulford site in Orient, New York. Harrington's (1954) date/bore size correlation chart, Binford's (1961) mean production date formula and Hanson's (1969) modifications of the Binford formula, the distribution of stems around the site, and the frequencies of bowl designs were some of the factors used to increase our knowledge of this site and its position in history.

Implications of Birth Order

As the oldest of three brothers I have always been interested in birth order. I created a survey which could show the different characteristics of the different birth orders. I used the χ^2 test to determine that there is a significant difference between the different birth orders.

The Relationship of Vegetation to Tide Levels in the Long Island Salt Marshes

The purpose of this project was to test the hypothesis that vegetation can reliably be used as an indicator of tide data levels and salt marsh boundaries. Using information from the National Oceanographic and Atmospheric Administration, the vertical distance data was normalized for mean high water.

Hydrogeochemistry of the Peconic River

This project studied the chemical content of the Peconic River to determine seasonal and spatial variations in a very unpolluted and undeveloped area. Water was sampled at seven sites along the river. An ion chromotograph was used to determine the concentrations of three anions: chloride (Cl^-), nitrate (NO_3), and sulfate (SO_4).

Cheating in High School: Definition, Extent, and Causes

This study attempted to assess cheating behavior and attitudes in a suburban high school, and relate them to several variables, including parental pressure, course level, and gender. It was found that 93% of students admitted to having committed, at least once, what are considered by administration to be major cheating infractions. A 1% level of significance was used to test the variables.

An Investigation of the Motivations and Pressures of Secondary Students in a Music Conservatory Preparatory Program

The objective of this project was to learn more about the backgrounds and motivations of musically talented youth. This goal was attained via the use of an anonymous survey and personal interviews which were given to students at the Pre-College Division of the Juilliard School of Music in New York, NY. Such topics as personal, peer, and parental pressures and relationships, ethnic background, socioeconomic status, and personal views on academics, music, and future career plans were addressed in the survey and the interviews.

The Effects of Family on the Decision-Making Processes of American and Japanese Students in a Moral Dilemma Paradigm

This study attempted to place American and Japanese students in a moral dilemma situation and compare the extent to which the family influenced how the stu-

dents responded, placed in that certain situation. It was found that Japanese students were influenced more by their family in making decisions than were American students.

Gender Difference in Everyday Knowledge
It has been found in other studies that women generally know less than men about politics (Jennings and Niemi, 1974). Since there are no significant differences in intelligence between men and women, the gender

gap in political knowledge has been explained by differing social expectations for men and women. Politics has been described as a "male" area. In the last twenty years there has been a change in American attitudes towards how men and women should behave. This study was done to see if the gender gap in political knowledge still exists among teenagers today.

Lyme Disease in Cattle: Characterization of the Immune Response and Evaluation of Serological Testing

Bovine sera from four states all had antibodies to the Lyme disease bacteria (*Borrelia burgdorferi*) as determined by enzyme linked immunosorbent assays. Certain of these cows with varying degrees of antibody reactivity were selected to have Western blots performed on them. Blot patterns from endemic and non-endemic areas were similar suggesting the immune response was not necessarily due to *Borrelia burgdorferi*. There was no correlation between amounts of antibody and the number of total bands for bovines used in this study.

STATISTICAL CALCULATORS

Solving statistical problems with just pencil and paper can often be a tedious task. Even if you understand the formulas, using them may be complicated and cumbersome when you have collected large amounts of data in a science research project. The following tools can help you perform your calculations.

SCIENTIFIC CALCULATOR

A scientific or graphics calculator can simplify working with large amounts of data. These calculators can be purchased for as little as twenty dollars. They can quickly sum columns of data, an operation frequently required in statistical formulas.

Most scientific and graphics calculators also come preprogrammed with many statistical functions.

Several of the important keys to look for when buying a calculator to use for statistical purposes are:

$\bar{x}$ sample mean
μ population mean
σ or σ_n population standard deviation
σ_{n-1} or s sample standard deviation
ρ population correlation coefficient
r sample correlation coefficient

     Scientific calculators are not difficult to use. A lit-
tle practice with the instruction book will save you
many hours of pencil-and-paper work.

COMPUTER PROGRAMS

Another time-saver is statistical software packages.
These programs are simple and easy to use. Most
people can load them and begin using them immediately.

     A computer program will do much more than the
scientific calculator. In addition to finding the values
for descriptive statistics, such as the mean, standard
deviation, and correlation, statistical programs will
allow you to determine whether or not the data you
have collected is statistically significant.

     The programs come with many statistical tests
for inferential statistics, such as the t test. Many of
them also have the ability to create charts, tables, and
graphs of your data.

SPECIAL SYMBOLS AND FORMULAS

Statistical formulas are filled with many symbols. However, most of the symbols are simply upper- (capital) and lowercase Greek letters.

USING Σ

The Σ symbol is found in many statistical formulas. This symbol, the uppercase Greek letter sigma, is a summation symbol. It is just a shorthand way of saying, "add up all the numbers."

Suppose you were given 10 biology quizzes in which the highest possible score was 10. If you listed the scores in your notebook, they might look something like this:

BIOLOGY QUIZZES: 8 3 5 9 7 8 6 4 10 8

You would probably give them some kind of title like the one shown so that you can identify them later. For convenience, statisticians identify their data with mathematical symbols instead of titles. Quite often, their title is a single letter. They might change your title to Q for quiz, but most likely, they will call it x for unknown. In that case, your list would look like this:

$$x: 8\ 3\ 5\ 9\ 7\ 8\ 6\ 4\ 10\ 8$$

This gives us the same information, but in a much more condensed form. You can now use the title much more easily with the summation symbol. Suppose you want to say, "add up all 10 quiz values." In mathematical form, that would look like this:

$$\Sigma x$$

$$\Sigma x = 8 + 3 + 5 + 9 + 7 + 8 + 6 + 4 + 10 + 8 = 68.$$

OTHER STATISTICAL SYMBOLS

Some other common symbols that are found in statistical formulas are listed below.

1. $\bar{x}$ represents the sample mean. It is read "x bar."
2. μ represents the population mean. It is the lowercase Greek letter mu, pronounced "moo."
3. σ represents the population standard deviation. It is the lowercase Greek letter sigma, pronounced "sig-ma."
4. σ_{n-1} or s represents the sample standard deviation.
5. ρ represents the population correlation coefficient. It is the lowercase Greek letter rho, pronounced "row."

6. r represents the sample correlation coefficient.
7. N or n represents the number of pieces of data that have been collected in the experiment.
8. χ^2 represents the square of the difference between a population frequency and a sample frequency. χ is the lowercase Greek letter chi, pronounced "ki," and χ^2 is the tested value in the chi-square test used in hypothesis testing.

USING STATISTXICAL FORMULAS

Mathematical formulas are just a way of writing complicated ideas in a mathematical shorthand. Two of the most often-used statistical formulas are shown below.

The Mean
The formula to find the mean is:

$$\bar{x} = \frac{\Sigma x}{n}$$

This formula says that to find the value of the mean:

1. Sum up the data values.
2. Divide the sum by the quantity of your data values.

A complete explanation of the mean is found in Chapter 2.

The Standard Deviation
The formula for calculating the standard deviation for a sample is:

$$s = \sqrt{\frac{\Sigma(x - \bar{x})^2}{n - 1}}$$

This formula says that to find the value of the standard deviation:

1. Find the value of the mean.
2. Subtract the mean from every data value.
3. Sum up these differences.
4. Divide the sum by the number of data values minus 1.
5. Find the square root of the entire calculation.

A complete explanation of the use and meaning of the standard deviation is given in Chapter 3.

Other Formulas Used in this Book

The formula for percentile rank (PR):

$$\text{Percentile Rank} = \frac{cum\,f}{n} \times 100$$

The formula for the range:

$$\text{Range} = \text{Maximum} - \text{Minimum}$$

The formula for the interquartile range (IQR):

$$\text{IQR} = Q_3 - Q_1$$

The Pearson r correlation coefficient:

$$r = \frac{\Sigma xy - \frac{1}{n}\Sigma x\,\Sigma y}{\sqrt{(\Sigma x^2 - \frac{(\Sigma x)^2}{n})(\Sigma y^2 - \frac{(\Sigma y)^2}{n})}}$$

The formula for the z test:

$$z = \frac{\bar{x} - \mu}{\dfrac{\sigma}{\sqrt{n}}}$$

The formula for the t test:

$$t = \frac{\bar{x} - \mu}{\dfrac{s}{\sqrt{n}}}$$

The formula for the ρ test:

$$t = \frac{r\sqrt{n-2}}{\sqrt{1-r^2}}$$

The formula for the χ^2 test:

$$\chi^2 = \Sigma \frac{(f_o - f_e)^2}{f_e}$$

TABLES OF
CRITICAL
VALUES

TABLE I. Critical Values of z

0.01 one tail	0.05 one tail	0.01 two tail	0.05 two tail
2.33	1.65	2.58	1.96

A one-tailed value can be either negative or positive.

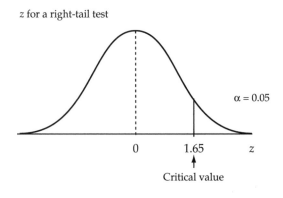

z for a right-tail test

$\alpha = 0.05$

0   1.65   z

Critical value

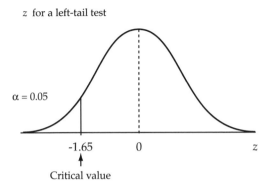

z for a left-tail test

$\alpha = 0.05$

-1.65   0 z

↑
Critical value

A two-tailed value is both negative and positive.

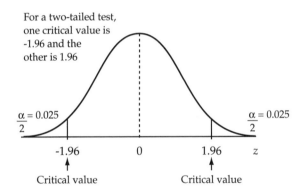

For a two-tailed test, one critical value is -1.96 and the other is 1.96

$\dfrac{\alpha}{2} = 0.025$ $\dfrac{\alpha}{2} = 0.025$

-1.96   0   1.96 z

↑   ↑
Critical value   Critical value

TABLE II. Critical Values of t

df	0.01 one tail	0.05 one tail	0.01 two tail	0.05 two tail
5	3.37	2.02	4.03	2.57
6	3.14	1.94	3.71	2.45
7	3.00	1.90	3.50	2.37
8	2.90	1.86	3.36	2.31
9	2.82	1.83	3.25	2.26
10	2.76	1.81	3.17	2.23
11	2.71	1.80	3.11	2.20
12	2.68	1.78	3.06	2.18
13	2.65	1.77	3.01	2.16
14	2.62	1.76	2.98	2.15
15	2.60	1.75	2.95	2.13
16	2.58	1.75	2.92	2.12
17	2.57	1.74	2.90	2.11
18	2.55	1.73	2.88	2.10
19	2.54	1.73	2.86	2.09
20	2.53	1.73	2.85	2.09
21	2.52	1.72	2.83	2.08
22	2.51	1.72	2.82	2.07
23	2.50	1.71	2.81	2.07
24	2.49	1.71	2.80	2.06
25	2.49	1.71	2.79	2.06
30	2.48	1.70	2.75	2.04
40	2.42	1.68	2.70	2.02
60	2.39	1.67	2.66	2.00
120	2.36	1.66	2.62	1.98
∞	2.33	1.65	2.58	1.96

TABLE III. Critical Values of χ^2

df	0.01	0.05
1	6.64	3.84
2	9.21	5.99
3	11.34	7.82
4	13.28	9.49
5	15.09	11.07
6	16.81	12.59
7	18.48	14.07
8	20.09	15.51
9	21.67	16.92
10	23.21	18.31
15	30.58	25.00
20	37.57	31.41
25	44.31	37.65
30	50.89	43.77

GLOSSARY

alternative hypothesis   the hypothesis that says there is a difference between the sample statistic and the population parameter.

average   a single number that represents a set of data. It is most commonly used to refer to the mean of the data, but it may also refer to the median or mode of the data.

bar graph   a graph consisting of either vertical or horizontal bars whose lengths represent the number of items in a category.

bimodal   describes a distribution that has two modes.

boxplot   a visual representation of a five number summary.

class interval   groups the data into separate categories to give an indication of the distribution of scores.

class mark   the midpoint of a class interval.

correlation   a relationship between two variables.

correlation coefficient a value between -1 and 1 that indicates the degree of relationship between two variables.

critical value in hypothesis testing, the value that determines whether the statistician accepts or rejects the null hypothesis. The location of the test statistic with respect to the critical value determines which decision will be made.

cumulative frequency the sum of all the frequencies of data values from the lowest class interval up to and including a given class. When divided by the total number of data values and multiplied by 100, it is equivalent to the percentile rank.

data the numbers collected and worked with during a science project. Some examples are: the number of french fries in a fast-food serving; the daily rainfall in inches; the age of Americans who have had heart transplants; and the height of sixteen-year-old girls in the United States.

decile breaks percentiles into 10 groups of 10 percentile points each.

degrees of freedom the size of the sample minus one.

descriptive statistic a measurable characteristic of data. Some examples are mean, range, percentile rank, standard deviation, and correlation.

distribution the way the data is spread over a range of values.

five-number summary a list of five numbers consisting of the minimum value, the quartiles, and the maximum value from a data set.

frequency the total number of times that a measurement or category occurs in a collection of data. The symbol f is used to denote the frequency of a measurement.

frequency distribution an arrangement of data that reveals how they cluster at various values. In other words, it offers an indication of how frequently the data appears in each section of a graph or table.

frequency polygon a graph made by connecting the midpoints of the class intervals.

histogram a graph consisting of bars whose length represents the number of items within a class interval. In contrast to a bar graph, the width of each bar represents a numerical value and the bars always touch.

hypothesis A hypothesis is a statement asserting the problem you will be investigating in your experiment. Some examples are: Is the age of heart transplant recipients getting younger? Are sixteen-year-old girls taller in 1996 than they were in 1956?

hypothesis testing a procedure statisticians carry out to test a hypothesis in order to determine whether data from a sample is representative of the entire population it comes from.

inferential statistic allows the researcher to make inferences about a population from studying a small portion, or sample, from it. Some examples of inferential statistics are the z test statistic, the t test statistic, and the p test statistic.

interquartile range the difference between the first and third quartile in a data set.

level of significance the probability of obtaining a type I error in hypothesis testing. It is a number the statistician chooses as an acceptable risk of error.

linear having a straight-line relationship.

mean the average of a group of data values found by dividing their sum by the number of values.

median the value of the central piece of data in a data set.

midpoint the value in the center of a group of data.

mode the value of the piece of data that occurs most often in a data set.

multimodal describes a distribution having more than two modes.

normal distribution a frequency distribution that when plotted has a symmetrical bell shape with the mean in the center and a specific standard deviation. This distribution is common for large sets of data.

null hypothesis the hypothesis that says there is no difference between the sample value and the population value.

one-tailed test a hypothesis test in which the rejection region is on only one side of the mean. In the geometric model, the rejection region is in only one tail of the distribution.

outlier a piece of data that is located far away from the rest of the data values.

parameter a measurable characteristic of a population. Some examples are: the average age of all the people in the United States who have had heart transplants, and the average height of all sixteen-year-old girls in the United States.

Pearson r correlation coefficient formula the formula for calculating the amount of linear correlation between two variables.

percentile rank the percentage of data that is equal to or less than a given value.

population all the individuals or objects with a common observable characteristic. Some examples are: all the people in the United States who have had heart transplants; and all sixteen-year-old girls in the United States. *See* sample.

probability the chance that an event will occur, as a fraction of 1, with 1 indicating it will definitely occur.

quartile breaks the range of percentiles into fourths.

random sample a sample selected in such a way that every member of the population shares an equal chance of being selected.

range the difference between the greatest and smallest values in a set of data.

sample a small group or subset of the population. Some examples of samples are: the people who have had heart transplants at your local hospital, and the sixteen-year-old girls in the tenth grade in your high school. *See* population.

skewed not symmetrical—slanted in one direction.

standard deviation a measure of the dispersion of data around the mean in a data set. In other words, it is a calculation that indicates how far the data values tend to deviate from the mean.

standard normal curve the plot of a normal distribution in which the mean has been set to zero and the standard deviation has been set to 1.

statistic a measurable characteristic of a sample. Some examples are: the average age of the people who have had heart transplants at your local hospital, and the average height of all sixteen-year-old girls in the tenth grade in your high school.

statistical significance the determination of whether a finding about a sample of data from a research project is valid from a statistical point of view.

student's *t* distribution a frequency distribution that occurs with small sample sizes. It changes shape with sample size, and at large sample sizes, it resembles the normal distribution.

symmetric describes a graph or set of values in which each half is a mirror image of the other.

true limits the upper and lower bounds of a measurement. The true limits of a number are equal to the number plus and minus one-half of the measuring unit.

two-tailed test a hypothesis test in which the rejection region is on both sides of the mean. In the geometric model, the rejection region is in both tails of the distribution.

type I error the error that occurs in hypothesis testing when a hypothesis that is actually true is rejected as false.

type II error the error that occurs in hypothesis testing when a hypothesis that is actually false is accepted as true.

whisker a line through the minimum or maximum value in a boxplot.

FOR FURTHER READING

Statistical Textbooks

Brase, Charles Henry, and Corrinee Pellillo Brase. *Understandable Statistics; Concepts and Methods.* D. C. Heath, 1991.

Moore, David S., and George P. McCabe, *Introduction to the Practice of Statistics.* W. H. Freeman, 1989.

INDEX